Joseph Michelli, Ph.D.

HUMOR, PLAY & LAUGHTER

Stress-Proofing Life With Your Kids

Joseph Michelli, Ph.D.

HUMOR, PLAY & LAUGHTER

Stress-Proofing Life With Your Kids

The Love and Logic
PRESSInc.

GOLDEN, COLORADO

Printed in the United States of America

Library of Congress Cataloging-in-Publication Data
Michelli, Joseph A., 1960-
    Humor, play, and laughter : stress-proofing life with your kids /
Joseph A. Michelli.
       p. cm.
    Includes bibliographical references (p.   ).
    ISBN 0-944634-49-4
    1. Parenting—Handbooks, manuals, etc. 2. Laughter—Psychological
aspects. 3. Wit and humor—Psychological aspects. 4. Joking
relationships. 5. Intergenerational relations. 6. Stress (Psychology)—
Prevention. I. Title.
HQ755.85.M53 1998
649'.1—dc21
                                          97-36458
                                             CIP

Editing by Linda Carlson, Louisville, CO
Design by Bob Schram, Bookends, Boulder, CO

ACKNOWLEDGMENTS

WHEN I SUGGESTED TO NORA that writing this book was like giving birth, she looked at me with a look I have come to know means, "You don't know what you are talking about." She is probably right. This labor of love was nourished by so many people who have touched my life, that a true accounting of them would be longer than the book itself. Rather than listing and inevitably missing many of those who have contributed to this work, I merely say thank you. I appreciate all from whom humor was shared, stories were told, parental advice was given, drafts were reviewed, words were edited, and patience was granted. I am forever indebted to each of you. May my endless droning about "the book" be over and the laughter and play resume.

DEDICATION

To Dad, Mom, Andrew, Fiona,

and grandchildren yet unborn.

May you rejoice in the laughter—

past, present, and future.

TABLE of CONTENTS

TAKING LIFE LIGHTLY

—Regina Barreca
Professor of English and Feminist Theory at the University of
Connecticut and author of *They Used to Call Me Snow White,
But I Drifted* and editor of *The Penguin Book of Women's Humor*

Perhaps it is true that angels fly because they take themselves lightly. Even if you might not feel a whole lot closer to heaven, you'll certainly feel the weight of the world lifted off your shoulders by reading Joseph Michelli's new book on the importance of humor and play in family life. I learned, for example, that toddlers laugh around 400 times per day; I also learned that this number dwindles to 16 laughs per day when adult life takes over. These are daunting statistics, especially when you consider that to come up with these numbers a whole bunch of psychologists sat around trying to count how many times a gang of toddlers giggled on any particular morning and compared them with, let's say, accountants on their lunch break.

But what Dr. Joseph Michelli does in his wonderful book doesn't depend on the transference of statistics or numbers, not even fascinating ones such as these. No, what Dr. Joseph Michelli has managed to do, almost magically, is to incorporate and translate major psychological and sociological theories of humor into his work and then—and this is the crucial part—put them to good use. Michelli makes ideas about humor accessible, usable, and funny in and of themselves. The ending of each section, for example, includes a number of activities under the heading "Open the Door and Let Humor In." These exercises encourage and challenge the reader to take an active role in the creation of play and laughter. Creative, clever, and constructive, these suggestions are difficult to resist. Prescribing laughter, literally and metaphorically, is exactly what the doctor orders to cure the personal and domestic blues.

"Families who laugh, last" is more than an aphoristically cute saying to be photocopied and plastered on the refrigerator with two thousand other assorted important pieces of paper (or plastered on the Internet, which Michelli suggests is a sort of world-sized fridge door). In creating this working blueprint for families who need to get more laughter into life (and can you name anyone who doesn't?), Michelli employs all his talents and gifts in an easy-to-open package.

Not only are there witty stories, jokes, and lessons along the way in this substantial and enormously readable volume—these we expect from a man who deals with humor, even when he's a well-respected clinical psychologist—but more importantly there are viable and realistic strategies for survival. We don't hear about the author's perfect life or perfect world; we hear about how he and his wife, Nora (who clearly deserves all the applause he sends her way), make their way through the raising of children, the coping with troubles, the everyday issues we all face.

That Michelli so freely offers his own history as a boy and teenager (experiences that all of us can relate to all too well!) in addition to detailing his experiences as a husband and parent makes his argument more persuasive than could all the charts and graphs in the world combined. I fully believe he has earned the right to laugh at the absurdities in life. His own experiences, for example, as the son of a mother who was always afraid she'd left the iron on (he took to carrying it with him, even on car trips) make him seem very much like "one of us," meaning someone who gets into terrible binds and needs to figure a sane way out of them. The stories he tells are proof enough of his theory that laughter and humor are potent ways to improve every life.

Exploring the uses of humor himself and—opening up for all his readers to see—talking honestly and wonderfully about his richly textured relationship with his wife and children, Michelli has achieved in this book what few authors can: a synthesis of the convincingly proven and the personally profound. By encouraging all families to nurture humor, play, laughter, and joy in their homes, Michelli is encouraging the most profound lessons and pleasures. Too often in today's culture family life is associated with stress, financial and emotional strain, worry, fear, and a sense of futility. Too often we hear stories about the mean parts of life, about strife so pervasive and so overwhelming that it hardly seems worth it to make an effort; worse, it sometimes seems sacrilegious to enjoy life at all while others suffer.

And yet what Michelli makes clear throughout his work—a work that confronts and copes with life's bad news as well as its good—is that to laugh even at our most trying experiences in no way diminishes the magnitude and importance of them. Laughter doesn't dismiss or disrespect our pain, but instead works to alleviate it, to put it into perspective, and to help us be able to cope in those situations when all our strength—from every source—will be called upon. Laughter, in Michelli's hands, is a gift we give ourselves, not something we take from others or use at the expense of anyone else. Like prayer, laughter is never inappropriate—unless you start to do it all by yourself, really loudly, on a city bus.

Even then you'll be okay if others around you join in. . . .

CHAPTER ONE

The IMPORTANCE of HUMOR

"The funniest things in life
are the unintended humor of reality."
—STEVE ALLEN

JUST AS I WAS GETTING THE HANG OF PARENTING our four-year-old son, Andrew, our second child, Fiona, entered the picture. With her arrival, I struggled through familiar nights of interrupted sleep and with my son's difficulties adjusting to another little person in the house. I could tell that Andrew was having problems, because he kept sneaking—as well as a four-year-old can sneak—into our bedroom in the middle of the night. He needed to be assured that his mother and I weren't going to forget him before morning. And he blatantly exclaimed that we now had one too many children in the house.

Prior to my leaving for an extended speaking tour, I told Andrew that I was concerned about his not being able to stay in his own bed. He appeared to understand that he could help his mother, Nora, capture precious sleep if he would remain in his room at night while I was gone.

When I returned from my tour, Nora met me at the airport with Fiona in her arms. An exuberant Andrew raced down the corridor of the airport and yelled at the top of his lungs, "Great news, Dad. No one slept with Mom while you were gone!"

How would you have reacted in that moment? Would you have scolded Andrew? Looked around nervously at the people who might have heard his remark? Laughed hysterically? Tried to clarify his outburst to strangers? How do you explain to 200 people in a crowded airport terminal that it's not what they think?

Realizing that Andrew was dealing well with change, and noticing especially his pride in managing that change, made me laugh with unmitigated joy. I hugged him tightly and congratulated him on his success.

Have you noticed how we frequently become so concerned with what we consider the "important" and "serious" aspects of childrearing that we ignore the absurdity and delight? We allow daily hassles to overshadow the joy and unintended funny moments that show up in day-to-day parenting. We concern ourselves with propriety and become so engrossed in the costly environment of our grown-up world that we overlook the free humor offered by our children.

When I mentioned to a friend that my wife was pregnant with our first child, he said, "If I had known you were thinking about having kids, I would have given you my boys for the weekend and ended for good all your desires to have children." Why is it that we preoccupy ourselves with the exhausting work of parenting rather than its opportunities to laugh and play? Of course there are challenges and hardships involved in the care of kids, but my friend failed to inform me of the joy, magic, and wonder that make having children such a consciousness-raising experience.

Organic humor—humor that occurs naturally—happens every day.
Willingness to attend to it is a significant component
of survival during stressful and painful moments.

BALANCING AWARENESS OF HAZARDS AND HUMOR

From birth we are trained to track danger. My well-intentioned parents left the house in the morning after unlocking five padlocks. They vigilantly patrolled their way to the car and anticipated the perils of driving. They knew they would be confronted by one of two seasonal hazards, winter or construction. They believed that other drivers intended to disrupt their day by driving too slowly in the fast lane or by failing to provide adequate braking space. As they dropped me off at school, they reviewed possible dangers and appropriate survival strategies: "Don't take candy from strangers. Only speak when spoken to. Don't let anybody bully you." And then, "Oh, by the way, have a nice day."

After school we rushed home for a quick dinner, which was followed by an evening of watching the news. First, my parents watched the national news to track all significant disasters throughout the world. Then we would view local news so that my parents could make sure they were not the only ones being picked on in their community. Finally, they had to watch a show like *Rescue 911* so they could intimately enmesh themselves in some disaster on the other side of the country that they otherwise would have missed. No wonder so many of us are on Prozac!

The danger messages of our childhood certainly have survival value. Failure to discuss appropriate reactions to the harm that might befall a child is clearly irresponsible parenting. But overemphasizing danger—especially without mentioning the importance of joy and mirth—is equally irresponsible. Teaching our children to be aware is essential. But why should we only teach them to be aware of life's hazards? Don't we also have the responsibility to help them become cognizant of joy and beauty? Shouldn't they also learn to open their hearts and minds to humor? Among other things, life consists of a balance between hazards and humor. Helping our children realize this balance not only helps them, it offsets our own experience with long-standing danger and fear messages.

Humor helps us to stop asking questions like: Am I being a good enough parent? What are other people thinking about me as a parent? How can a person so small have so much power over me? Rather than being fearful about our effectiveness as parents, we should exercise our ability to look for the funny aspects of parenting. When we find the joy in otherwise negative aspects of parenthood, humor helps us to step back and see the absurdity of a given situation and, if we're lucky, we laugh. Fear is manageable, and one way to manage it is with humor.

I once watched a parent in a mall use humor to handle the awkward circumstance of a child engaged in a loud tantrum. As people passed by and stared at the screaming toddler, the father said, laughing, "Don't worry. He's just practicing for a part in an upcoming horror movie." His perspective allowed him to be more effective in tending to his child, less fearful of what other people think, less concerned about his ability to parent, more at peace with the situation, and able to laugh.

When we gain control of our fears—
which we can do with humor—we discover that we can
exchange paralyzing self-doubt for creative problem-solving.
And we teach our children that they can do it, too.

A child once told me that when he is laughing, there is no room in his brain to be scared. I couldn't have said it better.

ATTUNING YOUR SENSES

No matter how humor-impaired you think you are, let me give you hope. Whether you believe you have defective humor genes, have an overly serious perspective on life, or have lived through a devastating childhood, you are curable. Opening your eyes and ears to the humor around you is an important first step in experiencing a full recovery. The long-standing theory that "laughter is the best medicine" is no longer merely theory. Scientific research has shown that humor and laughter build more flexible minds and healthier bodies. How satisfying to know that the power to bring joy and happiness into our lives is actually ours!

Comedians have long known how to tickle our funny bones, but each of us is able to self-medicate with laughter when we need it most. I don't know about you, but for me that would be during some of the more challenging hours of parenting. I want to help you learn how to laugh at yourself and to teach your children to laugh at themselves, too. It is my hope that this book will help you become aware of the daily wealth of joy and humor in parenting that awaits you—no matter who you are, where you are, or how busy you are.

I hope you will be encouraged to understand and teach your kids the important part that humor and laughter can play in daily life and to see how merriment can help everyone face and learn to manage stress. One day your children may be parents themselves, and you know they will need all the help they can get.

MEASURING YOUR ABILITY TO PLAY

Conditioned by parental messages and the cruel adolescent humor we grew up with, many of us learned to fear humor. Tired of being the butt of jokes or anxious that someone would poke fun at us, the last thing we wanted was to draw attention to ourselves by being silly. As a result, during our maturation process, we became contaminated with rigidity, which decreased our joy and curiosity. I refer to this contamination process as abject adulteration (AA).

Is there a cure? Yes, by increasing our silliness quotient (SQ). The remedy involves examining strategies for reenergizing our willingness to play and be silly without fear of how it looks to the neighbors. Increasing our silliness quotient (SQ) corrects for the harsh aspects we learned during the maturation process. We will renew our sense of childhood play—a sense that was corrupted by some of the more disheartening aspects of growing up.

Remember intelligence quotients? IQs were calculated by first measuring your mental age, as determined by your score on a test of intelligence. That score was then divided by your actual age and the result multiplied by 100. For example, if your mental age is calculated at 20, and you are actually 10 years old, you would divide 20 by 10, resulting in an answer of two. This multiplied by 100, would indicate that your IQ is 200, which, by the way would be considered the score of a genius.

Your SQ is even easier to determine. Take your actual age, subtract the age you act when you are playing with children, and multiply by 10. For example if you are 35 and you act 35 when you play with kids, your SQ would be zero ($0 \times 10 = 0$). If, however, you are 35 and you act 10 when you are playing with children, you would have an SQ of 250, reflecting the score of a true play genius.

An extra 250 SQ points are available if you can maintain your childlike state when you are outside the presence of children; and still another 250 bonus points can be yours if you sustain that state in the presence of another adult.

With this formula, advancing age has its advantages, particularly if you maintain your sense of play. When I recently calculated the SQ score for my 75-year-old father, who consistently plays with Andrew at Andrew's five-year-old age level, he achieved an impressive SQ of 700.

*The willingness to recapture silliness is a growth process—
an exercise in putting aside expected adult behavior.*

Humor is frequently referred to as a "sense"—similar in a way to taste, touch, vision, hearing, or smell. As a sixth sense, here's what humor can do:

❖ *Minimize distorted perception of danger;*
❖ *Help manage anger more effectively, thereby reducing conflict;*
❖ *Provide breathing room for constructive, loving, and logical decision-making;*
❖ *Assist in communicating difficult feelings;*

❖ *Enhance feelings of well-being;*
❖ *Augment creativity;*
❖ *Strengthen social relationships;*
❖ *Abate the physical ravages of stress;*
❖ *Create a home environment of warmth and joy.*

Given such benefits, it seems to be a sense worth developing. Humor skills are not bulldozers designed to clear the roads of unwanted problems, but they can provide shock absorption for the bouncy ride. In the pages that follow, you will see how play and laughter can become tools to help us cope, heal, become more flexible, prepare for unexpected transitions, and broaden perspective—all valuable equipment for life's journey.

Open the Door and Let Humor In

1 ACTIVITY ONE...
Open Your Senses to the Humor Around You

With at least one other family member, take a good look at the occurrences of the day and name three funny things that happened.

    1. What was the funny occurrence?
    2. What was funny about it?
    3. What did you discover about your family member listening to this situation?
    4. Where will you look for humor tomorrow?

2 ACTIVITY TWO ....
Carry a Disposable Camera

Since joyous occurrences can unfold in a moment, why not carry a disposable camera to capture them? You could carry one in your glove compartment, purse, or briefcase and forever preserve the precious memories of your life.

3 ACTIVITY THREE..
Find Your Silliness Quotient (SQ)

Spend an hour with your child and take turns being as silly as you possibly can be.

    1. Use the silliness quotient to measure your silliness level:

✢ What is your actual age?
✢ How old did you act while playing with your child?
✢ Subtract your play age from your actual age.
   Multiply by 10.
✢ What is your silliness quotient?

2. What did you do to be silly?
3. What made these things funny?
4. Do you think this activity enhanced your relationship
   with your child? If so, how?

CHAPTER TWO

PLAY IS a FREE LEARNING TOOL

*"You can discover more about a person
in an hour of play
than in a year of conversation."*
—PLATO

RECENTLY, Andrew expressed some frustration as I was leaving for work. Rather than rushing to defend myself, I listened to his concern. He said, "Dad, why don't you take the day off and spend it with me?"

For a fleeting moment, I actually considered his request. I thought about the fun we could have. In seconds, I came to my senses about the realities of life, but at least I didn't give him the lecture my father would have given me. That story was about walking for miles through snow without shoes, which was somehow supposed to relate to the importance of hard work.

Instead, I asked, "What would we do if I could stay home?" I was impressed with myself. I marveled at the caring and open quality of my question. No father—no psychologist—could have done better. I listened as this delightful little boy, without any forethought, went on and on about what we could do. In just a few moments, I was learning a lot about how my child's mind works, what he loves to do most, and how he envisions a perfect relationship between us. Granted I did not find all his suggestions exciting, but some of them certainly measure up to what I would consider a day well spent. And listening to him for just a few moments, I imagined what we both could learn if we actually did spend the day playing together.

My self-congratulation began to wane after 10 minutes of Andrew detailing plans for our day. He finished by saying, "So now that you know what we're doing, you can't go to work!" How was I going to break the bad news to the little guy, now that I had aroused his hopes? I had the sinking feeling that my well-intentioned question had served to increase his expectations of me rather than diminish them.

Thinking as quickly as I could, I looked around his room and began to point to things that my going to work enabled him to own. Before I finished, Andrew said, "Dad, aren't you going to be late?"

Other than the handful of people who actually believe they are experts and write books on the subject—and we all have our doubts about them—no one knows how to parent. If we were to tell the truth, we'd have to admit that we fake our way through the process at least half the time. It is as if we are walking a tightwire for the first time. Humor and play, however, provide a net when the going gets tough.

PARENTING: YOUR CHILDREN ARE NOT YOUR CHILDREN

With modern technology providing many twists on what it means to be a parent—including surrogate mothers and cloning—and with legal battles raging between birth parents and adoptive parents, a definition of parenting may be less obvious than it once was.

Kahlil Gibran wrote:

Your children are not your children. They are the sons and daughters of life's longing for itself. They come through you but not from you, and though they are with you yet they belong not to you.

You may give them your love but not your thoughts, for they have their own thoughts. You may house their bodies but not their souls, for their souls dwell in the house of tomorrow, which you cannot visit, not even in your dreams.

You may strive to be like them, but seek not to make them like you. For life goes not backward nor tarries with yesterday. You are the bows from which your children as living arrows are sent forth. The archer sees the mark upon the path of the infinite, and He bends you with His might that His arrows may go swift and far. Let your bending in the archer's hand be gladness; for even as He loves the arrow that flies, so He loves also the bow that is stable.[1]

Gibran reflects the daunting job description of parenthood, which includes maintaining your own stability, acting in gladness as you love and guide your children—without controlling them, without reducing them to copies of yourself. Of course, Gibran doesn't talk about being wise and sane in the face of last-minute school projects, disputes about who called whom what name, and the need for designer tennis shoes, which will be outgrown before the credit card statement arrives. His job is to inspire, and inspire he does.

I think we can agree for our purposes, however, that parenting is the art, skill, and commitment necessary to raise a child to become a functional adult.

HUMOR: SOMETHING TO KEEP IN BALANCE

Great thinkers across time have long pondered an appropriate definition for humor. Some people believe that humor is indefinable since no two people experience it in exactly the same way. What may be funny to you may be repulsive to me. Despite differences in terminology, many modern humor theories still share elements that date back to the ancient Greeks.

What makes things funny? Ancient philosophers and modern psychologists alike believe:

❖ *The Uncomfortable Theory*. Funniness arises when we express feelings about things that give us a sense of discomfort, such as sexual urges or aggressiveness.

❖ *The Incongruity Theory*. Humor allows us to be amused when we encounter the unexpected. What we hear sounds incongruous to our ears.

A friend was discussing with her first grader the source of various types of animal products. She asked, "Where does bacon come from?" And her daughter said, "From a pig." My friend asked, "Where does milk come from?" And the girl said, "From goats and cows." "And where does hamburger come from?" asked her mother. Not missing a beat, the young girl said, "McDonald's."

The incongruity theory is at work in the young girl's response. We were expecting to hear "cows," and the girl's response fit neither her earlier responses nor our expectation.

The word *humor* comes from the Latin word *umor,* which means to be fluid or flowing. According to the understanding of physiology held in earlier centuries, there were four basic bodily humors (or fluids)—and an unattractive group they were:

MELANCHOLY. An abnormal state attributed to an excess of black bile and characterized by irascibility or depression, or pensive mood.

CHOLER. The state of being marked by or suffering from disordered liver functions and excessive secretion of yellow bile, causing a peevish, ill-natured disposition.

BLOOD. The seat of the emotions, an overabundance of which makes for a showy, foppish person.

PHLEGM. Considered to be cold and moist and to cause sluggishness, intrepid coolness, or calm fortitude.

The four humors were thought to significantly affect a person's mood and disposition. Whereas a normal temperament involved a balance of these bodily humors, an excess of any of the humors was an indication of grave disturbance.

In 1560, Laurent Joubert, a French physician, wrote *Treatise on Laughter*, in which he explained why the eyes shine and tear during laughter. "The eyes sparkle in joy because they are full of clear and glistening humors which shimmer as they take flight, everywhere seeking an exit, just like a bird in a cage."

The Greek philosopher Aristotle thought that laughter assisted in getting a person's humors in balance. People with their humors in balance were viewed to be in "good humor." Individuals who could see the absurd in the world and make others laugh were viewed as humorists.

We are frequently faced with the task of balancing our children's humors. It can happen anywhere. Once, I watched a mother struggle to comfort her crying daughter in the waiting room of a doctor's office, but to no avail. When a nurse suddenly emerged donning a bright red clown nose, the child's demeanor changed instantly. I am certain that no amount of reassurance from the girl's mother would have been as effective as the nurse's unexpected and well-timed playfulness.

LAUGHTER: A POWERFUL FORCE

How do we define laughter? The physical experience is one in which the brain reverberates and electrical waves surge through the body. Chemicals are released through the pituitary gland, and body temperature rises. Vocal chords quiver, pressure builds in the lungs, and the face contorts in anticipation of the 70-mile per hour breath that erupts from the mouth. And you thought when you laughed you were simply having a good time.

Laughter can result from having a funny experience. Or, it can result from being anxious or tickled, which have nothing to do with humor at all. But whatever its cause, it has rewarding physical and emotional benefits.

The sound of laughter is like a ray of sunshine in a dark room.
It is the universal language of happiness
that reflects no dialects and needs no translation.

Shared laughter strengthens the bonds of family and friendship. It punctuates positive experiences and enhances a group's solidarity. How much easier is it for children to engage a laughing and smiling parent than an angry or depressed one? Laughter discharges tension, eases conflicts, deflects hostility, and helps create an environment that feels safe.

Play: A Path to Learning

If I ask you the opposite of black, you are likely to say white. If I ask you the opposite of happy, you are likely to say sad. If I ask you the opposite of work, you will likely say play. But play is more than the opposite of work. Play is any activity that lacks a defined purpose prior to initiation but provides significant purpose through participation.

For children, play is equivalent to work. Children don't feel it's work, but, play is their work. When we observe children playing, they seem to be involved but with no distinct purpose. On closer review, however, it becomes clear that play lures children into learning. They are drawn to activities that pleasure them and, unbeknownst to them, help them master essential skills.

For example, when a two-year-old merrily pretends to have a conversation on a plastic phone, he is enhancing his language skill development. When a three-year-old roars off on her tricycle, she is developing advanced motor abilities. When a ten-year-old kicks a soccer ball with friends, he is broadening his physical skills and developing his social skills at the same time.

Play allows children to freely experience the world
with no predetermined goal,
but in the process they learn about the world
and how to make their way in it.

Once we let go of goal-oriented, purposeful activity we enter the world of play. Therein lies its paradox: The act of letting go and playing provides us with skills that give us greater control over our work.

Although some may think their children play too much, I say that as adults we play too little. Our participation with children in play not only aids in their development but allows us to experience their excitement and pleasure firsthand.

Play actively:
+ *Strengthens family unity;*
+ *Reduces destructive behavior;*
+ *Increases a sense of responsibility;*
+ *Diminishes television and video-game addiction;*
+ *Improves school functioning; and*
+ *Aids self-esteem.*

All this, without having to do any work.

A father I know confirmed that when he finally involved himself in consistent playtime with his daughter, they were able to form a meaningful relationship. He hadn't realized that play would bridge the distance between them.

> *Play is the most effective way to talk with children.*
> *Rather than telling them what to do,*
> *we can connect with them in nonthreatening ways*
> *via the comfortable sharing of thoughts and feelings.*

Our interactions in play teach pertinent rules of social conduct as well as problem-solving skills. Most importantly, play enables children and parents to bond, and to do so with foolishness and abandon.

As I looked out the window recently and saw my wife and son making mud pies, it was difficult to see where Andrew left off and Nora began. Of course, I had seen through my wife's adult disguise long ago. In this moment, I couldn't tell the child from the parent. With mud-smeared hands and a beaming face, Nora had suspended her adult image and was experiencing Andrew from his eye level. Her silliness quotient was at an all-time high.

Humor, laughter, and play are not only important for our children's long-term development but also for our sanity as we probe the minefields of parenthood. The next time you are caught playing with your child and someone accuses you of wasting time, grab this book and blame it on me. At last, you can justify reliving your childhood. There, now. Aren't you ecstatic that you have children?

Open the Door and Let Humor In

4 ACTIVITY FOUR ....
The Joy List

Joy is an emotional state similar to happiness but tends to be a more fleeting experience of pleasure. When a sense of joy consistently exceeds a sense of sadness, a person is likely to view him- or herself as happy. A joy list can help us get in touch with the happiness that surrounds us. I keep a running log of things that bring me joy and add to my list every day.

Flipping back through my list randomly, I come across number 610, written after the family had spent several days at Disney World. While we were there, we repeatedly heard a prerecorded announcement during stage shows that said, "Please remain seated during this performance. The use of video cameras or flash photography is prohibited." Several days later Fiona stood up in her stroller, and Andrew cautioned, "Please be seated in your stroller. The use of flash photography is not allowed." What a wonderful phrase for us to use anytime a child is doing something you would prefer she not do. Everyone instantly understands the caution of danger, and everyone gets to laugh at the same time.

The joy list records your family's moments of mirth and fun. It can be as simple or elaborate as you choose. Write down in a blank notebook any funny incidents that occur in your family.

When I first made the decision to keep a joy list, it seemed that joyful things were hard to find. Like learning any skill, learning to track joy can be slow and full of starts and stops. Remember learning to ride a bike? Same process. Overcoming awkwardness takes nothing more than time. Begin your joy list today. Take a few, quiet seconds and list one or two aspects of your life that bring you happiness. No editing allowed.

5 ACTIVITY FIVE ....
Family Humor Album

If you want to go a bit further, keep a scrapbook of pictures and stories. You can appoint one member of the family to be your family humor historian or you can all take turns. It can be fun to record different family members' perspectives of a particular story. Call it "Family Views of the Same Story." Enjoy both the process of creating your journal and the pleasure you derive in looking through the pages together.

Andrew recently wrestled with me and feigned an injury to his left ear. Infatuated with bandages, he returned to the battle zone with a bandage on his right ear. When I informed him that he had doctored the wrong ear, he took the bandage off and returned to the medicine cabinet. I surmise that he became confused again while in the bathroom. In an effort to cover his bases, he placed Band-Aids on both ears. A photo of my son in such a state is in our humor album with a brief narrative covering the joy this experience brought.

Many photos of our family crowded into photo booths, making silly faces, are included in the album as well. I also carry a few of these photos in my wallet and pull them out occasionally when I need to remind myself not to take things too seriously.

6 ACTIVITY SIX ....
Silly Human Tricks

You've probably seen David Letterman's segment called "stupid pet tricks." How about capturing your family oddities through silly human tricks. Maybe it's Mom's ability to touch her nose with her tongue, or Baby's aptitude for miraculously squirming out of her clothes while both fists are full of chocolate chip cookies. Every family has them. Make the most out of these familial absurdities. They are your family's free entertainment. Hold a Silly Human Tricks audition session or talent show with your own master of ceremonies.

CHAPTER THREE

A NEW WAY to COPE

*"The Constitution guarantees the American people
the right to pursue happiness. You have to catch it yourself."*
—BENJAMIN FRANKLIN

IF YOU ARE LIKE MOST PARENTS, the ride home from the hospital
with your newborn is rich with emotion, filled with the joy of
your child's arrival blended with an overwhelming sense of
the responsibility you have for the proper care of your child.
Beyond the short-term concerns about late-night feedings and
the demands of a totally helpless being, most of us worry about
how our parenting will affect our child's future.

I remember going to a first-time, expectant father's group
when Nora was in the third trimester with Andrew. After the
group facilitator established that I was the only participant who
had not been signed up by his wife, he decided that I should
tell my story first.

I started by saying that I was afraid I might not be a good
father. I questioned whether my child would grow up to be
happy. Would his life be filled with strong, gentle tailwinds, or
would he be pelted by unrelenting, gale-force headwinds?
Would he be able to respond to life's adversities with joy and
creativity, or would he resign himself to hardship? What would
help him find joy, peace, and happiness? Wealth, intellect,
material possessions, and a childhood devoid of crises? Or a
childhood rich with disasters to help him develop coping skills?

As I finished my emotional purging and looked around the room, I had the distinct feeling that this was not the right place to become so vulnerable. The group leader asked the other men to comment on my opening remarks. In essence each of my so-called peers reported that they didn't know what I was talking about. Most of them insisted they had no fears about father-hood and claimed that they had come to learn all the basic skills they would need—like changing a diaper.

When the group members later discovered that I was a psychologist they seemed to give me a knowing look, as if to say, "That explains everything." Well, I had an explanation for their behavior as well: Pure, outright denial.

The other group members were not open to admitting it, but most of us dedicate a considerable amount of thought and concern to our children's long-term emotional development. We hope that our parenting will model for them the skills they will need to survive, develop, and find happiness in an increasingly complex world. Humor, laughter, and play won't correct for flat-footedness, but they have shown promising effects with short-sightedness. The way that humor can give your children a chance to catch the America dream is by helping them cope with life's nightmares.

THE RAVAGES OF STRESS

The complexity of the world today is harrowing with various studies suggesting:

❖ *There are approximately 2,000 teenage suicides annually;*
❖ *One-third of school children under age 18 use illegal drugs;*
❖ *More than a third of children suffer stress-related illness, including wheezing, headaches, and stomach difficulties;*
❖ *As many as 15 percent of high-school students are problem drinkers;*
❖ *School dropout rates hover around 40 percent;*

❖ *One in 10 teenage girls between the ages of 13 and 17 becomes pregnant each year; and*

❖ *One-third of all violent crime is committed by people under age 20.*

We could have a lengthy discussion regarding why these statistics exist. Our world has grown into a complex structure, and so many children are not getting the attention they need. They are not being given the skills they need to adjust to the challenges of today's world—perhaps because adults are in the throes of working out those skills themselves.

Dr. Bettie Youngs, in her book *Stress and Your Child*, comments on children's inability to cope with stress at school:

Instead of children who are happy and have a zest and zeal for living, learning, and playing there are signs of emotional duress too obvious too miss. . . . Aren't children supposed to be joyous, energetic and mischievous? Where has all that gone? Why are so many children showing signs of anger or apathy, or both? Why are so few of these young people laughing and learning? Why are youths inflicting violence on fellow students? Why are they living what seem to be lives of quiet desperation? Why are children's lives so stressful? [2]

A popular definition of stress is "anything that threatens us and requires us to adapt." This definition assumes the following thought process:

❖ *I perceive that a threat exists.*

❖ *I need to cope with this threat.*

❖ *How do I cope with it?*

EXAMINING THE "FIGHT-OR-FLIGHT" RESPONSE

The most natural human reaction to fear is the "fight-or-flight" response, which is activated within us when we feel threatened. It has existed as long as humans have existed. When we are threatened, the stressor registers in the hypothalamus, causing a secretion of adrenal hormones and resulting in an increased heart rate, increased blood pressure, decreased blood flow to the periphery of the body, and decreased digestive functioning. And that's the abridged version.

There are two basic ways we respond when we are frightened: One is to fight; the other, to run away. If you think for a moment about a situation in which you felt scared, you may have wanted to lash out at someone or something or simply run and hide. In more primitive times, stress befalling humans included the appearance of, or an attack by, wild animals or aggressive mongrel tribes. These creatures posed real threats to humans' physical survival. When faced with these dangers, humans would either fight the creatures or run from them.

Today, for the most part, we have eliminated these ancient physical dangers. Although there are an inordinate number of injuries sustained by violence in the streets, most stress we deal with today is symbolic or psychological. We see a movie with dinosaurs and have nightmares. We hear a television news program report about a violent occurrence and fear that it will happen to us.

We perceive situations as dangerous when we don't have control of the events of our day—our child refuses to get dressed, the car won't start, the project deadline has been moved up a day, a power outage disables the TV, VCR, computer, garage door opener, and fax machine. Although this lack of control in no way threatens our survival, we still feel stressed. We want out of these situations. We want to fight the teacher, the boss, the family member, the system—verbally or physically—or we want to run away from them and never have to deal with them again.

As each new stressor activates our fight-or-flight response, we burn adaptive energy as we prepare to either fight or run away. Because our fight-or-flight readiness energy is finite, our ability to adapt begins to suffer.[3] Over time, continual activation of the adaptive system results in psychological stress. Such burnout can contribute to a variety of physical problems. Some people develop migraine headaches or cardiovascular disease; others suffer hypertension and ulcers.

There are two goals in managing stress that can take us beyond fighting or running away—mentally and physically:

1. Reduce the number of things you perceive as threatening. For example, perceiving a person as an enemy does not help you manage stress. Change your perception and you change your level of stress: That person is not an enemy; he is someone who has a different opinion, who needs help, who has a problem. Maybe I can help him. Even if you do nothing more than think these thoughts, the threat, as you perceive it, will decrease.

2. Increase the number of ways you can act. Managing stress constructively is critical to survival. It provides children alternatives to destructive or escapist behaviors when their stress levels are high. Show your children that every action they take requires a decision on their part and that they are capable of such a decision. Furthermore, they need not react to others but always have the option to act as they see appropriate.

It is essential to teach our children that the search for satisfaction is not an external one. It comes from making appropriate decisions from within and acting in accordance with a chosen perspective.

The real pursuit of happiness is a journey inside ourselves—
a quest that involves trusting our innate ability to learn,
understand, and shift our perspective on life if need be.

SPACE TO THINK AND TIME TO COPE

It has been said many times, but the saying still holds true: It does not matter what cards you are dealt in life but how you play the hand. As adults we understand that we don't have control over certain cards we are dealt—who the IRS audits, who wins the lottery. But we do control how we react to the events in our lives and whether we react to the undesirable events with a playful spirit or with anger and despair. If we respond to life's difficulties with hopelessness or anger, we diminish our problem-solving abilities. We also succeed in pushing others away from us. Conversely, if we can respond to adversity with understanding and humor, we augment our ability to solve problems and come up with workable solutions, and people tend to stick around to help.

A client of mine claims that his mother always laughs when things go wrong. "At first I thought my mom was touched. Now I know that she provided me the ability to choose hope in the face of crisis." My client seems to suggest that by using humor, we can stop time and create distance. When you laugh in the moment, or joke about a situation that has just occurred, you give yourself two amazing gifts—space to think and time to cope.

In that moment of laughter, you can think about how you are going to respond:

❖ *Will you react to the situation in the same way you always have?*
❖ *Will you act the way you were taught is proper?*
❖ *Will you act from a new perspective?*
❖ *Will you react defensively, or act from an objective point of view?*
❖ *Will you choose hope in the face of your crisis?*
❖ *Will you stop and think about the outcome of your action?*
❖ *How would you want someone to react to you if you had initiated this circumstance?*

All of these questions can be answered in the space of that moment you create when you stop time, create distance, and take a breath by using humor.

Children learn to find the glass half full rather than half empty by watching us and listening to us. From birth our children hear our words but are keenly attuned to our behavior. Living a life filled with laughter and play offers them optimism, flexibility, and joy. It corrects for social nearsightedness and alters their vision of the world from one that is uncontrollable to one that is magical, hopeful, and fun.

Most pessimists believe that a negative expectation is a healthy one, because it better prepares you for the worst—if it should occur. In reality, pessimism consumes a person's perspective over time, forming a rigid, negative view of life—a habit that is, in fact, difficult to break. When a person expects a bad outcome and that outcome does not occur, the pessimism is not weakened. Rather, with each setback, each negative expectation proves to become self-fulfilling. If you expect to be depressed, you are more likely to make choices that will depress you. The human mind works in wondrous ways.

But even a die-hard pessimist can learn optimism through humor, laughter, and play. Of course, true pessimists would doubt this.

The Joy of Play vs. the Pain of Losing

I observed a nine-year-old boy called "out" while he slid into second base during a Little League baseball game. The boy immediately jumped to his feet, threw his helmet to the dirt, and started to scream inches away from the umpire's face. Within moments his father, rushing from the stands, was right beside him engaged in identical behavior with the umpire. Watching the father, I saw that the acorn had not fallen far from the tree and better understood the child's need to be verbally aggressive toward the umpire. He had learned from his dad that it's not how you play the game, but whether you win or lose that counts. The child hadn't learned the joy of play—only the pain of losing.

I conjured up an image of Fiona sliding into second and being called "out." She would take pride in the slide, enjoy getting her uniform dirty, and would probably tell me that she was glad she was out because it saved her having to run the rest of the way around the bases.

Open the Door and Let Humor In

7 ACTIVITY SEVEN ....
Silly Songs

Materials needed: A voice—any voice

What could be more joyful than a song? In our home, music is for play and certainly not an art form. Why not enjoy a rousing round of "It ain't gonna rain no more, no more, it ain't gonna rain no more. How in the heck can I wash my neck if it ain't gonna rain no more?" for the pure silliness of it?

There are many wonderful children's tapes if your own repertoire is limited. A company called Wee Sing⁺ has a great selection. If your kids are older or tired of the standards, make up new lyrics to old songs. The lyrics can humorously deal with your family's challenges. I'm certain that Weird Al Yankovic started this way.

8 ACTIVITY EIGHT ....
Dress-Up Trunk

Materials needed: Cardboard or storage box, a variety of dress-up clothes.

Little girls and boys love to dress up. There are many places on this earth where you will see that a lot of adults never quite grow out of that phase either. As a family, you can start collecting varied articles of clothing in an assortment of sizes. Obviously, the wackier the better. Garage sales, Goodwill, and the Salvation Army can be wonderful sources for that special piece of fur or hat you've been searching for—and at a good price. Collecting a comic wardrobe is fun in and of itself.

Use your dress-up clothes for impromptu plays or tea parties. A friend of mine told me how she painted her child's chicken pox with calamine lotion. When our son came down with chicken pox, Nora remembered a smock and beret in the dress-up trunk. She concocted a mini-palette, donned smock and cap, and became Vincent Van Go-Away. Not only did the calamine soothe Andrew's poor body, the crazy artist soothed his soul.

Another friend of ours found an old military hat and pair of plastic handcuffs. When his children are caught in an obvious lie or dereliction of duty—such as dirty laundry all over the floor— he apprehends the subject. Speaking with an atrocious accent, he returns them to the scene of the crime. He reports fewer power struggles and a lot of laughs. Use clothing that doesn't match to hit the peak of the laughter meter. We found that our baby, Fiona, in full beard and me in a pink tutu are real winners.

9 ACTIVITY NINE..
Hilarious Holidays

Materials needed: Homemade calendar, a little imagination

Make holidays of your very own. Create a new set of holidays just for your family. Come up with a list of original holidays. Place them on dates throughout the year. Make sure you follow through and celebrate your new holidays. Here are some examples:

Topsy-Turvy Day. Wake up and keep on your pajamas. Have a lovely supper (instead of breakfast)—maybe pizza or spaghetti. Stay in your pajamas in the morning and loll about the house doing evening activities. Have breakfast for dinner and then put daytime clothes on to go to bed. You can add your own special touches.

You-Be-Me Day. Parents get to be kids and kids get to be parents. Enough said. You figure out the rest.

CHAPTER FOUR

AN Rx for HEALING

"The art of medicine is to amuse the patient
while the disease runs its course."
—VOLTAIRE

T HANK GOODNESS my children don't have far to fall because they fall a lot. After having spent an entire weekend in the emergency room with two unrelated cuts, one for Andrew and one for Fiona, I realized a whole new meaning to "leaving them in stitches."

Whenever my children are hurt or unhappy, I find myself more concerned with their enjoyment of a long and happy life. Did you know that stress can lead to physical as well as mental maladies? Since 50 percent of all illness is lifestyle-related, I am reminded of how important it is to help our children learn how to decrease the physical ravages of stress and enhance the functioning of their immune systems. My favorite way to do this? By playing and laughing.

DEVELOPING A ROBUST "AMUSE" SYSTEM

These days we are all aware of the importance of maintaining a strong immune system. As I see it, an essential contribution is the development of a robust amuse system, one that has significant stress-resistant qualities, which benefits health and longevity. How can we help our children challenge life's stressors? By teaching them to deal with the stressors. First, we should remind them to take space to think and time to cope. Then, they should ask themselves some key questions. Asking the right question can pacify and clarify a situation in an instant. Here are some examples.

Will I remember this in five years? This is one of my favorite things to ask, because in the face of what looks like a disaster, this question often puts me immediately in touch with the fact that I may not even remember this so-called disaster in five days, let alone five years. It's a reality check, and it never fails to calm me down. Sometimes it makes me laugh outright.

Wouldn't I be laughing if this were happening to someone else? I love this question because the fact is, I would. No disrespect to my friends, but when I think of my disaster happening to them, I laugh—not so much at them as at life. Humor distances me from a fight-or-flight response and challenges me to decide whether such an event deserves to be viewed as a threat.

Is this worth dying for? No. Hopefully, the answer is almost always no. It's become difficult these days to spot danger. Because of violent movies and frightening news broadcasts, we tend to view everything as potentially dangerous and life-threatening. It's important to be on guard and prepared, because life-threatening situations do happen, but if we lose our sense of humor, we lose our sense of balance.

To stress or not to stress? That is the question. Sometimes I have to do a lot of work to convince myself not to choose stress, but when I acknowledge that I have the choice, I start to believe it. Believing is the first step to sanity. I take a few deep breaths, get myself in balance, and look again at the situation before me. It only takes a few moments to find the balance again. Take those moments. They will save you time down the road.

What did we do in the days of the Pony Express? These days, with the aid of technology and an individual's ability to communicate with another person almost instantly, we tend to view all situations of our lives as emergencies. I noticed that once I was reachable by e-mail, fax, cellular phone, and pager, everything needed to be done more quickly. I have patients who page me in the middle of the night because they cannot sleep. They are threatened by their confusion over their appointment time for the next day. Just as people disagree on a definition of humor, I sometimes disagree with my patients on what qualifies as urgent.

Asking yourself how important or dangerous a situation is prevents you from responding to every alleged crisis by either fighting or running away, both very natural reactions to a threatening situation.

Using humor to create time and distance keeps you in the moment. Staying in the moment enables you to stop, think, and then act, based on a clearheaded decision, instead of simply reacting.

I have a friend who retires to her room for quiet time each day and has spent considerable time and energy educating her 11-year-old son about acceptable and unacceptable reasons to disturb her. She has instructed him that if it is bleeding and won't stop, burning and not extinguishable, or ticking and not defusable, she can be disturbed. Anything else can wait for the twenty minutes that she takes for relaxation.

A PRESCRIPTION FOR LAUGHTER

If we use humor to let go of threat, no crisis alarm needs to be sent through the body. Through the miracle of laughter, our bodies return to normal functioning after a fight-or-flight alarm goes off. Laughter signifies to the brain that all is well and that there is no cause for distress. Furthermore, not only does laughter produce an alternative to fighting or fleeing, it exercises our heart muscles and contributes to overall physical health.

American humorist Arnold Glasgow said, "Laughter is a tranquilizer that has no side effects."[5] Laughter not only melts away the pain of rejection, hopelessness, and despair; it also helps us resist disease.

Lee Berk, Ph.D., and Stanley Tan, M.D., both of Loma Linda University, were among the first to study the physical benefits of laughter.[6] Their work and that of colleagues indicates that laughter decreases the production of the stress hormones cortisol and epinephrine and increases production of upper respiratory antibodies, enhancing the activity of T-cells and lymphocytes to attack tumors and viruses. So chicken soup may no longer be the only known remedy to help with the common cold. Have you ever had a doctor write you a prescription for laughter? Here's one for you now:

> **Rx**: *Laugh 100 times a day as loudly as you can.*
> *No need to call me in the morning.*
> —DR. JOSEPH MICHELLI

Laughter has also been shown to assist body functions other than the immune system. Norman Cousins, a champion in the field of health and laughter, referred to laughter as "internal jogging" because it works the cardiovascular system by improving circulation and increasing heart rate. One of the pioneers in research on the physical benefits of laughter, William F. Fry, M.D., from Stanford University, says: "Laughing 100 times a day is the cardiovascular equivalent of 10 minutes of rowing."[7] As we laugh, our lungs draw in more oxygen and we eliminate carbon dioxide more efficiently.

As a medical psychologist, I have worked with children in burn units who were obviously in too much physical pain to laugh. Many were able to fight through their emotional suffering and find, as Br'er Rabbit would say, their "laughing place."

When they did, they found—within the world of their thoughts, memories, and imaginations—that they could resist focusing on the threats their bodies were experiencing. They were able to settle, even briefly, into a mental place of laughter that felt safe and comfortable. Being in their laughing place provided them relief from pain and improved healing and tissue regeneration. Mark Twain knew what he was saying when he uttered so simply, "Nothing erases unpleasant thoughts like pleasant ones."

Andrew, Nora, and I spend a lot of time talking about Andrew's laughing place, and we will do the same with Fiona as she grows up. Andrew knows this place exists inside of him and that he can call upon it, even if laughter is not possible, as was the case when he was bitten in the face by our family dog. His laughing place is created by using some quick mini-visual imagery. He closes his eyes, smiles, and takes a trip to Disney World in his mind, seeing himself looking at all the rides. In this special place, there are no lines and everyone there is his friend. He has complete access to any ride he wants. In the amusement park in his mind, he laughs and laughs, and he knows that nobody can take this place away from him.

The Natural High of Endorphins

When I first heard the word *endorphins*, I thought they must be children without parents who stay indoors. Sorry. Actually, endorphins are any of a group of proteins with potent analgesic properties that occur naturally in the brain. Long-distance runners often talk about feeling a natural high when they've been running awhile and no longer feel any pain in their muscles. When endorphins are released, that's exactly what happens. You feel no pain.

The word *endorphin* comes from the merging of two other words—*endogenous* (self-produced) and *morphine* (one of the world's most powerful pain killers). "Runner's high" is an example of what can occur when endorphins are released through exercise. Of course, I experience no endorphin release when I run, probably because I don't do it very often. Instead I get the experience of lactic acid pumping pain into my underused muscles. I refer to this as "runner's low."

Laughter apparently fights pain by triggering the release of endorphins. When a person laughs, muscle tension increases initially then relaxes. And it doesn't produce the muscle stiffness that many associate with exercise.

Maybe the next generation can come home from work and choose a laugh instead of a drink or a cigarette to relax. Such a choice would create untold benefits to longevity— and reduced risk for cancer as well as heart and lung disease.

New techniques for measuring the electrical activity of the brain have shown that when people listen to jokes the entire cerebral cortex (outer layer) is involved. Since laughter is considered a whole-brain phenomenon, there is speculation that it may increase coordination between the left and right hemispheres.

COPING STRATEGIES AROUND THE WORLD

In other countries, laughter is viewed to be of such importance to health that laughing clubs have been created. In India, where at least eighty of these clubs exist, people come together to laugh—usually at dawn. They raise their arms to the sky and—rather than share jokes—they simply begin to laugh aloud and expose themselves to the laughter of others. Whereas in the United States we see people walking, jogging, running, or practicing Tai Chi in a park, in Bombay we may come upon people wearing Keds, saris, turbans, or sweatshirts, laughing their way to health. Do they know something we don't?

In an effort to determine whether humor skills affect longevity, George E. Valliant, M.D.,[8] participated in research that followed people's health behavior over several decades. His research examined the relationship between specific personality factors and the long-term health status of individuals having these quali-

ties. He was primarily looking for personality factors that predict-
ed "hardiness" or disease-resistance. He identified five psychological coping strategies that he calls "mature defenses." What he
found was that of those individuals, aged 55, who had used
mature defenses throughout their lifetime, 80 percent were in
excellent health and 20 percent had minor health problems. Of
those who did not use mature defenses, 33 percent were in good
health, 33 percent had minor health problems, and another 33
percent were either dead or disabled by age 55.

In general, the five coping strategies are:

❖ *Find a clear purpose for living;*
❖ *Anticipate the logical consequences of your behavior;*
❖ *Learn to let go of anger and guilt before they become*
  rage and shame;
❖ *Use humor regularly; and*
❖ *Respond to negative emotions with creativity.*

Find a Clear Purpose for Living. People who have a clear sense
of purpose for their lives and believe their lives have meaning
can withstand a considerable amount of stress if they are convinced that the stress serves a greater good. People who have a
clear sense of purpose for a particular activity that is meaningful
for them can endure a considerable amount of pain, if the pain
serves a greater good, for example, the pain of childbirth.

Anticipate the Logical Consequences of Your Behavior.
Individuals who anticipate the logical consequences of their
behavior are more likely to resist disease throughout their lifetime.
Clearly, if you cannot anticipate the consequences of drug usage,
violence, or unprotected sex, the consequences can be fatal.

**Learn to Let Go of Anger and Guilt Before They Become Rage
and Shame.** What strong emotions they are—anger, guilt, rage,
and shame. And what havoc they wreak on our bodies.

Individuals who used emotional reactions like anger and guilt positively—to motivate themselves to confront their own behavior or the behavior of others—were found to have excellent disease-resistance. Those who held on to rage and shame had their physical health compromised.

Use Humor Regularly. The use of humor as a defense is both subtle and refined. Humor permits us to express what we feel without causing discomfort or immobilization, and without having an unpleasant effect on others. We can unload without obliterating, instruct while entertaining. Humor removes the need to put forth a false front, and it provides an outlet for feelings that, expressed another way, could be destructive.

Respond to Negative Emotions with Creativity. There are many choices for dealing with negative emotions. For example, when your child has a temper tantrum in a public place, you can choose a number of different ways to respond. One is to get angry and yell at him. Another is to tell people in the grocery store that he's studying to be an opera singer. Which do you suppose would relax you more?

What simpler and better way to encourage our children to be healthy than to help them discover and develop their humor perspective? In the course of their discovery, they become more flexible, insightful, and prepared to live in this world.

In the chapters that follow, we'll take a closer look at the specific kinds of humor that appeal to certain age groups.

Open the Door and Let Humor In

10 ACTIVITY TEN ....
Find Your Laughing Place

Finding your laughing place is simply a matter of finding a space inside you where you can conjure up some laughter. It's a place that provides at least temporary relief from discomfort.

1. Get into a comfortable position. Close your eyes.
2. Take slow, cleansing breaths. Focus on the richness of oxygen filling your lungs and the release of tired air through your nostrils and mouth.
3. As you do this, allow yourself the luxury of closing out competing thoughts. Any interruptions you experience are mere thoughts, and you can decide whether to attend to them now or later.
4. Imagine that you are listening to the sounds of a cool, trickling stream, or perhaps feeling the warm sensation of a breeze being propelled from a forceful wave.
5. Take a few minutes to think about places that have consistently provided you with smiles, laughter, safety, or contentment. Allow yourself to remember the location, people, and colors. Allow yourself to experience the specific aspects of this place—how it feels, what sounds you hear, scents you smell, things you can touch.
6. Choose a perfect place. Feel free to change it any way you desire. Remove extraneous people or add something that makes you feel joyful.

When someone in your family is in pain, ask that person whether he or she can find his or her laughing place. If so, everyone can laugh with that person. If the person finds it impossible to laugh in that moment, be sure he or she understands that that's okay, too.

Know that you need not indulge your laughing place only during formal relaxation exercises, but that you can also use the images as mini-stress busters while standing in the express checkout lane at the supermarket behind a man with 46 items and an out-of-state check.

11 ACTIVITY ELEVEN ....
Fight, Flight, Laugh

Conjure up a situation in which you have experienced stress. Tell other family members what that situation was. Next, imagine that the situation were happening right now and share:

1. What would you do to fight the situation or any person involved in the situation?
2. What would you do to get away from the situation or any person involved in the situation?
3. What action could you take instead of fighting or running away?
4. Would any of these other actions be humorous?

12 ACTIVITY TWELVE ....
Joy Jar and Pearl Pot

Materials needed: Jar or box, paper strips, pencil

The joy jar is similar to the joy list. Have the family sit down together and write on paper strips specific activities, places, and things that brought everyone in the family pleasure. Store them in the jar. Every once in awhile, take out a strip and bring back the joy.

The pearl pot can hold "humor pearls" created by the family. Each pearl is a piece of wisdom from members of the family:

"Remember. Today is the last day of your life—so far."
"A trip of a thousand miles begins with a cash advance."

When someone around you is need of humor, pull a joy strip from the jar or a pearl of wisdom from the pot.

CHAPTER FIVE

FIRST SIGNS of LAUGHTER

*"Life as a close-up is a tragedy,
but as a long-shot is a comedy."*
—CHARLIE CHAPLIN

A FRIEND and her 18-month-old daughter were in the greeting card section at a drugstore. My friend was looking at the cards while her child was taking them out of the rack, throwing them on the floor, saying "Uh-oh!," and laughing. Occasionally her mother would pick up the mess and return to peruse more cards. Suddenly, her child's laughter gave way to a cry for help. The call came from the next card aisle. As my friend turned the corner, she saw a pile of undamaged cards on the floor and her daughter being detained by a store employee. Relieved that her daughter wasn't hurt, the mother began to laugh. The employee insisted that this was not a laughing matter and that he saw where the child had learned her "bad behavior." Mother and child laughed as they were escorted from the store, likely banished until they could be "good" again.

The store employee might have been afraid that he would have to pick up the cards and put them back. He probably had enough to do and didn't need the extra work. However, I cannot help but think that he had lost his sense of humor somewhere between being a child and becoming a grown-up. It's unfortunate that he couldn't have laughed with them, since the mess had already been made, and the child was too small to understand anything except that she was having fun. Don't you think the store employee would have felt better if he had been able to laugh?

Humor skills give us the flexibility to pull back the cameras from viewing close-ups of our lives long enough to see the absurdities that abound on the sides of the stage.

Over the years we have discovered that there are specific kinds of humor that tend to appeal to certain age groups. Perhaps you have tried to make your child laugh and have inadvertently used humor that appeals to a child much younger or much older. Humor can be puzzling in that way. If something makes you laugh, it doesn't necessarily follow that the same thing will make your child laugh—and, of course, the same is true in reverse.

THE NEWBORN—REPETITIVE SOUNDS AND TACTILE SENSATIONS

Our amusement barometers are wired into our nervous systems. A newborn baby smiles in response to physical touch (rubbing stomach, or stroking face) that is accompanied by a favorable sound, such as a mother's voice. By the second month, the infant's smile spreads into a warmer grin that occurs in response to a wider variety of events. As a child becomes more aware of her world, she smiles at sights, sounds, and touches that interest and please her. Lights, moving objects, and familiar faces all produce grins in an infant.

One common experience that pleases babies is for you to look directly at them. Eye-to-eye contact assists the baby in focusing his eyes for longer periods and is part of the earliest social response. A gentle tickle to a baby's tummy or chin is typically responded to with pleasure. In the 6- to 12-month range, babies are responsive to the "Where's the Baby?" game in which you hide your face and ask, "Where's Baby?" Then you show your face again and say while smiling, "There he is."

Classic activities like "Pat-a-Cake" and "Rock-a-Bye, Baby" offer repetitive sounds and predictable tactile sensations for the infant. Mirrors can be used with infants at this age to help them experience the tactile and perceptual differences between touching a person and touching a reflected image. Infants also respond to general conversations directed toward them with a wide range of vocal tones and emotions.

Infants often experience pleasure when they are exposed to different tactile objects, such as sponges, brushes, fur, and feathers, or to the dramatic visual contrasts of facial expressions, such as pictures of people with happy and sad faces. Panting like a dog, pretending to drink from a cup, or interacting with the child by clanging old pots and pans together or playing "this little piggy went to market" while touching her toes all serve to give her pleasure.

Most babies begin to actually laugh aloud by the time they are nine weeks old, with some infants showing signs of laughter as early as 29 days. Initially, surprise or a certain feeling inside the infant prompts the smile or laughter response. By four to six months of age, an infant responds to sounds and touch with obvious delight. As the infant develops, laughter is linked to the combination of sound and physical stimulation. Kissing your child's stomach and tickling his ribs while saying, "I'm gonna get you," fuel the laughter of your developing infant.

By eight months, the child frequently laughs in response to parent-instigated "peek-a-boo." Eight-month-olds also laugh in response to unusual behaviors of adults, such as a parent crawling on the floor. At approximately 10 months, an infant actively responds to the funny and comical faces of parents and other adults. A mother sticking out her tongue, wearing a mask, or walking funny will prompt a one-year-old to laugh.

One-year-olds are more likely to laugh at unusual behaviors on the part of adults if the children are in a safe environment and are familiar with the individual making the face. Strange faces and strange environments will prevent the very same behavior from provoking a laugh.

New parents struggle as their baby cries in its first months of life, and they try to guess what each cry means. The baby cries, the parent checks the diaper. The baby keeps crying, the parent attempts to feed the baby. The baby keeps crying, the parent walks the baby. The baby keeps crying, the parent begins to cry. However, when the baby begins social laughter, usually sometime near the end of its first year, the parent knows exactly what the child is communicating—pure joy and delight in her parent's presence. This delight serves as a building block for the bonding that continues between the parent and the child, ensuring that the child's future learning experiences come easier.

THE SECOND YEAR—FOCUSED GAZERS AND PROVOKERS OF LAUGHTER

After a year, children begin to initiate laughter for themselves and their parents by playing peek-a-boo or making silly faces. The child focuses on the eyes and mouths of its caregivers. One mother told me that she was amazed at how steadily her child would fix his gaze upon her, as if he were studying every centimeter of her face.

An infant looks to the face of his caregiver to get critical information about his or her world. The caregiver's face signals to the child that he is safe and cared for. The facial and vocal information communicated from the parent and received through a genetically preprogrammed system in the child produces the child's sense of security and contentment. Just as wolf cubs respond instinctively to differences in the sounds of their mother's howls and squeals, so does a human infant respond to subtle differences in the facial expressions of his or her parent.

As the toddler learns to provoke laughter, the laughter mounts and mounts, increasing from once an hour at age 16 weeks to once every four minutes at age four years. I certainly can't find that many things to make me laugh. But I've been learning from Andrew. Andrew laughs when I get lost. He laughs when his sister mispronounces a word. He laughs when he's surprised. He laughs when Nora uses a funny voice.

*I have learned a lot about how amusing the world can be
by spending time seeing it through my preschooler's eyes.*

TODDLERS AND PRESCHOOLERS—EXPLORERS OF SYMBOLIC PLAY

The toddler's ability to see that one item can symbolize another usually occurs early in the second year of life. Symbolic or "as if" play occurs when the child can take an object such as a book and use it "as if" it were a table. As they engage in symbolic play, they simultaneously begin to understand the humor that can result from such play.

Toddlers and preschoolers investigate things that are mundane to adults—such as boxes, labels, and dirt. They also explore the most annoying things in life, like the volume control on your radio, the meaning of the word *no*, your ability to shop effectively, and the limits of your patience.

A child's ability to "make believe" and symbolically represent his world opens him to a greater appreciation for silliness. It expands his vision of life's unexpected events. I watched a preschooler laughing to himself with delight as he used a bath towel "as if" it were a cape. He flew through pretend lands and saved imaginary civilizations from certain extinction. If you have children, you understand immediately that sometimes a towel is not just a towel.

I can't count the number of times I have had to clarify for Andrew that "This is not funny. I am angry." But I have to admit that Andrew is right. I caught myself in the mirror once, and when I am angry I *do* look funny. Certainly, I am concerned enough about the way I look when I am angry to not risk sharing it with strangers. Like any good husband and father, I like to save it for the ones I love.

*On the average, toddlers laugh approximately 400 times per day.
Sadly, by the time we become adults,
we have reduced our laughter to a meager 16 times a day.
Of course, we don't have to go quietly into the adulterated abyss.*

I set goals to increase my daily laughter and keep track of my progress along the way. I am nowhere near 400 laughs a day, but thanks to Andrew I am gaining on 100 most days. By laughing more and laughing loudly, I encourage my children's laughter as well. I had a friend tell me that he couldn't remember having heard his father laugh. This is not the tragic legacy I would like to leave. In fact, I would like my tombstone to read: "Here lies Joseph A. Michelli, who laughed to death."

I have tried to share my favorite jokes with Andrew, however, he seldom finds my jokes funny. For example, I was extremely proud of the following joke that I shared with him.

I asked Andrew, "Why did the lion spit out the clown?"

Andrew said, "I give up."

I said, "Because he tasted funny."

Andrew was unimpressed, probably too young for wordplay humor. I assumed he lacked the verbal skills to understand the double meaning associated with tasting "funny." A joke that fails likely reflects a problem on the part of the listener and not necessarily a weakness in yourself as a joke teller, or in the joke itself.

A FULL EXPRESSION OF EMOTION

The diminishing rate of laughs from toddlerhood to adulthood is a rather subtle and unintended cost of learning to live in society. The type of humor presented by toddlers and the increasing social responsibilities placed on parents to tame their wild offspring both serve to reduce laughter. I watched a father try to quiet his children's laughter in a playground because "they were making too much noise." If their joyful noise was not okay on a swing set, then where? Although children screaming in public can certainly be annoying, their laughter seldom distresses others. Instead, laughter tends to be contagious. Rather than suppressing our children's laughter we may want to revamp our own perspectives. Why not view their laughter as a way to rediscover the laughing child within ourselves?

Many of us have only one set of experiences to draw upon when raising our children—the ways our parents treated us. Although our parents may have been excellent, we are forced to rely on hazy memory to recall our childhood experiences. No one told us we would be tested on them later when we were adults. To further the confusion, social messages and values change with time.

When it comes to the humor memories of our childhood, some of us heard, "Wipe that smile off your face!" or "Grow up. Act like an adult." As if the laughless adult condition was something a joyful child would want to emulate.

I particularly remember hearing statements like these when I was six years old and had locked my father in our garage for fun. The more frustrated he became, the funnier the situation seemed to me. From his point of view, I should have acted more like an adult, since no self-respecting adult person would find humor in a situation like this. Or would he?

Nora tells a story of how her parents would send any child caught laughing at the dinner table up to their room "to practice laughing." Although Nora would accept her banishment quietly, her sister Reggie's laughing could severely disrupt dinner not only for her parents but for neighbors as well.

I have done an accounting of the messages I received as a child. These messages greatly affect my response to my own children's humor. Even for someone like me who is intent upon increasing the silliness quotient of my household, past negative messages sometimes get in the way of fully encouraging my son's and daughter's humor development.

Occasionally, I find anti-humor messages from my past flying from my mouth as if I were momentarily possessed. These messages, in turn, lodge deeply in the recesses of my children's minds and await their opportunity for expression. I fear that someday I will hear Fiona quoting me as I have quoted my mother. She will turn to her daughter and say, "What do you think is so funny? You may be laughing now, but you won't be laughing for long." On the other hand, I do hope that Fiona encourages her children to dance, make music, and sing, as her grandmother encouraged me to do.

If an infant fails to receive adequate touch, as well as intellectual or emotional stimulation, there is a risk that the child will not bond with its caregiver. Connecting with children by smiling and laughing is essential to bonding. I am convinced that if a child's smiles and laughter are ignored, the child can be damaged for life because of a failure to bond.

If we are not provided ample opportunity to see a full expression of emotion on the faces of those who care for us when we are infants, then, as we mature, our ability to understand the emotions of others may be hampered. Empathy is based on an ability to understand the emotions of others and to take those emotions into consideration when we act in the world. A significant component in the development of antisocial or criminal behavior is thought to be linked to problems with empathy and attachment. Our prisons are filled with adolescents and adults who have failed to positively attach to their caregivers.[9]

Open the Door and Let Humor In

13 ACTIVITY THIRTEEN ....
Bonding

Create a sound and touch to use with your newborn child. Is there a vocal sound that's soft, pleasant, and playful that you can come up with? What is a touching exercise you can do with your child? Rub his tummy? Tickle her arm while you talk to her? What about your own form of "peek-a-boo"?

As you plan to spend a certain amount of time with your child every day, keep in mind that your newborn will respond to sound, touch, and sight. From age one on, you will be spending time with provokers of laughter. Prepare to laugh together, and laugh a lot. Choose an activity where you can be eye-to-eye.

14 ACTIVITY FOURTEEN ....
Rediscovering Laughter: Celebration Strut

You've seen it a million times. Football players do their own special strut after scoring. Basketball fans jump up and down slapping hands yelling, "Yes! Yes!" after a particularly great slam. Little children gesture excitedly on Christmas morning as they unwrap that special toy.

Start by just paying attention to how other people celebrate. Pay attention to how you react to good news. What do you do when you're even a little happy? What does your face look like? What do you sound like? What ways does your body move?

Create your own individual celebration strut and have each family member create their strut too. Feel free to add sounds and movement. You can even create a "Family Celebration Strut"— one that involves a sequence of behaviors and sounds involving all family members (perhaps start with the tallest and go to the smallest). The sky is the limit.

15 ACTIVITY FIFTEEN ....
Lunch Box Surprise

Materials Needed: Notes, cartoons, silly objects

Andrew came home one day and told Nora that a lot of the kids at preschool got notes in their lunch boxes (you know, that mushy stuff) which were read aloud by the teacher. He wanted her to start sending him notes as well. Nora did this for awhile and then branched out to sending knock-knock jokes, funny pictures, and silly little gadgets or small, inexpensive toys that might tickle his funny bone.

School-age children love this humor enhancer and you can vary the humor depending upon their age. A friend of Nora's even started sending jokes and little comics along with her husband's lunch. One day she forgot to send something along, and it made for a tough afternoon for his coworkers.

CHAPTER SIX

SYMBOLS of JUVENILE and ADOLESCENT HUMOR

"Time spent laughing is time spent with the Gods."
—JAPANESE PROVERB

I REMEMBER VIVIDLY a Catholic funeral presided over by Father Allen. My 12-year-old friend Tim and I were altar boys. He was a year older than I, therefore more mature. Actually, I believe the maturity IQ of preadolescent and adolescent boys decreases in direct proportion to the number of boys present. For example, one boy with an IQ of 100 equals 100, two boys each with IQs of 100 equals a total IQ of 50. You are in for real trouble when 10 or more boys are present at the same time.

Returning the incense burner to the table during the funeral, Tim spilled hot coals on the carpet. He reached instinctively for water to put out the fire, but what he grabbed was holy water— water blessed by the priest, thought to have healing powers. Partly because the holy water, of all things, was not effectively dousing the fire and partly out of fear that the funeral might take on larger proportions, I began to laugh. As I laughed, Tim laughed. As Tim laughed, I laughed more. We were fledgling, laughing firefighters caught in a most inopportune moment.

After saving the congregation—which is how we saw it—we were dismissed from the altar to the back row of the church for the remainder of the service. We sat ever fearful and completely humiliated as each mourner exited past us. I don't remember hearing any praise from Father Allen concerning our rescue efforts or our ability to see the humor in an unusual situation. Instead we heard about the disgrace our laughter would bring our families. I was sure the lead story on the evening news would be, "Michelli boy laughs as the fires of hell rage."

While I understood why Father Allen talked to us about the inappropriate timing of our laughter, I believe it would have been more helpful if he had acknowledged our anxiety in the situation and suggested other options for handling it. We had obviously learned about the excesses of our behavior by experiencing the natural consequences that ensued. Looking back on that time now, I think how wonderful it would have been if he had acknowledged that the scene was truly funny and that God gave us laughter for a reason. We still would have been embarrassed by the situation, but we certainly would have experienced more peace of mind. The situation has given us a story to tell, which as funny as it seems now, terrified and mortified me then. Sadly, no positive spiritual messages about laughter were offered, although many were available.

Within the oral tradition of some American Indian tribes, it is believed that the greatest gifts we can give to one another are a smile and a laugh. Church reformer Martin Luther said, "It is pleasing to the dear God whenever thou rejoicest or laughest from the bottom of thy heart." Obviously, Father Allen would not have subscribed to these beliefs. I cannot help but wonder how our laughter would have been handled if Tim and I had been members of an Indian tribe.

GRADE SCHOOL: WORDPLAY AND THE FORBIDDEN

As children grow older, their expanding mental abilities alter the things they perceive as humorous. Whereas infants find a funny face worth giggling about, older children's developing language skills cause them to find wordplay and puns particularly humorous. As children master language, the challenge of wordplay diminishes. By the time they are adults, they are likely to greet puns with "aarghs" rather than laughs.

From an early age children realize that the forbidden is humorous, and they quickly become experts on making parents uncomfortable. Sometimes I think it's just so they can elicit strong reactions from us, which, of course, they perceive as funny. This represents nothing but trouble for most adults.

My hard-to-please son was impressed with one joke, primarily because of its forbidden nature and the impact it had on me each time he told it. Consistently, his telling of the joke provoked an "Oh, Andrew," an "aargh," or a "hush" response from his mother or me.

For a grade school boy, the ability to provoke a strong response in an otherwise calm adult demonstrates the true power of a joke.

Andrew showed his uncanny ability to tell the joke by identifying the most forbidden time for its delivery—at a party at my boss's home, with his proud parents' hand on his shoulders. Andrew confidently stretched out his hand to my boss and, by way of greeting, he uttered the stem of his favorite joke.

"Do you know the difference between broccoli and boogers?" he asked my boss as his mother and I froze like deer hypnotized by headlights in the surrealistically slow moments that followed.

My boss dangerously responded, "No, what?"

Masterfully, Andrew delivered the punch line, "I don't eat my broccoli."

As soon as Andrew's words left his mouth, his eyes fixed on the cascade of colors emerging on our faces. Our hands dropped from his shoulders. We stepped back. My wife and I exchanged looks that indicated our shared view: He inherited this from your side of the family. Most importantly, Andrew was entertained, and once again the joke was a keeper.

Andrew similarly found our reaction funny when we intro-
duced him to a friend of ours, the meteorologist on a local television news program.

Nora told Andrew, "This is Mike. He's the weatherman on
the television news each night."

Andrew boldly responded, "I hate weather."

Of course, our efforts to explain to Mike that Andrew didn't
mean what he said only made things worse.

Children and adults of all ages laugh at forbidden topics.
Obviously, what is forbidden for Andrew (boogers) differs from
what is off-limits for me (sex), but forbidden topics create
humor because they produce discomfort. Many marginal comedians make a living utilizing obscene and vulgar humor. They
capitalize on producing laughter by increasing—and then
resolving—tension. Other comedians find truths about the
human condition, which they reflect to us in amusing and
laughter-provoking ways, that need no tension for effect.
Forbidden humor may produce an easy laugh, but frequently
it does so at someone's expense. Mae West, the legendary sexy
movie star, once said that "it's hard to be funny when you have
to be clean."

Children are affected in diverse ways,
and so easily influenced when they are young.
New people, new thoughts, and new feelings fascinate them.
They are impressionable and vulnerable.

THE COMPANY THEY KEEP

Freud suggested that all humor reflects aggressive or sexual
urges. One would think that he spent a lot of time with adolescents.
As children age, influences on their humor development expand.
Other children, teachers, spiritual leaders, and friends all play a role
in establishing the types of humor and acceptable limits children
place on them. Teachers are becoming more aware of the value

humor has in the intellectual and social development of children. Of course, this doesn't mean your child's teacher prizes children's humor. Sometimes this is with good reason, since children have been known to use humor negatively against teachers. Children may use humor against any authority figure who presents them with a threat, but this is learned behavior.

A client told me she noticed that when her 10-year-old boy spent time with her male friend, her son would become increasingly sarcastic and use humor against her. This led her to restrict associations between the two and ultimately to ending her friendship with the man. When I asked if this was an extreme sacrifice, she explained, "I try to minimize my child's exposure to people who might harm him. People who don't know how to use humor appropriately are dangerous."

This has certainly caused me to consider the humor health of people who have regular contact with my own children. While humor in early childhood tends to serve the child's need for exploration, adolescent humor appears to be more involved in distinctions among people, helping children to develop a sense of identity separate from their parents. For this reason, adolescents, caught in a difficult age, often attack those who don't conform.

One of the frustrations with adolescent humor is that it frequently uses a sarcastic tone. It generally targets parents, adults, and authority figures but also plays to group identity, making "outsiders" feel like aliens. Adolescent humor often reflects cruel defiance.

JOKE-JITSU AND CONFLICT MANAGEMENT

The challenge of finding appropriate humor never ends as children grow and develop, continually defending their newly forming identities. Children of all ages face unkindnesses, but the cruelty is obvious in this statement I overheard a teenager make to a supposed friend. He said, "A brain is a terrible thing to waste; particularly for the donkey who gave up his for you."

If a child can disarm conflict with humor, he decreases the need to use physical or verbal aggression to resolve differences. President Ronald Reagan had great skill with humor in conflict management. During his re-election campaign, he was asked by a surly reporter if his advancing age would affect his ability as president. Not missing a beat, Reagan said, setting up his joke, "Andrew Jackson was 75 years old and still vigorous when he left the White House." Then he delivered the famous punch line: "I know, because he told me." The ability to undermine the hostility of the media by bringing the joke back on himself was one of the endearing qualities of President Reagan's social persona.

Each of us has the capacity to soften social conflicts through self-directed humor. These conflict deflection skills have been referred to as joke-jitsu, since they work on a principle central to the martial art of jujitsu. In this style of combat, a person redirects the attacker's momentum back toward the attacker. By letting go and rolling with the punch, the person being attacked causes the force of the assault to create a reverse flow that actually harms the aggressor. Similarly, letting go of resistance to a verbal attack through humor can disarm the intended aggression.

Recently, I saw a child use joke-jitsu very effectively. Two girls were playing with dolls, when one said, "Your dolls are ugly." The other responded without hesitation, "All the more reason they need someone to play with them."

A person's ability to laugh at herself is a desirable trait. Some have suggested the desirability of self-directed laughter is a result of too few people actually doing it. Generally, we attempt to present ourselves in as positive a light as possible. Nevertheless, most of us have accepted that we are not perfect. Self-directed humor allows us to acknowledge our imperfections. Laughing through one's weaknesses reflects self-awareness and self-acceptance.

Given that children will tease one another, self-directed humor takes away the power of the person doing the teasing. It would be hard to imagine making fun of Jimmy Durante's nose, Arnold Schwarzenegger's accent, or Jay Leno's chin.

When we are willing to admit our weaknesses through humor,
we increase the likelihood that others will admit theirs.

At a minimum, our willingness to be humble decreases the
need for others to become defensive around us and actually
draws their support. If the primary focus of humor is ourselves,
people don't need to fear that we are going to put them down.
Did you know that the custom of shaking hands began as a
means of demonstrating that a weapon was not being held?
Self-directed humor works the same way. It indicates that we
bare no intent to injure or harm.

Self-directed humor helps us accept our limitations to a
greater degree. Once we acknowledge our inability to make
decisions readily, speak in front of groups effectively, or run
quickly, we have uncovered the fear and anxiety attached to
the weakness. If this weakness is a personal demon and we
can make the demon funny, it loses its ability to torment us.

GUIDING YOUR CHILDREN'S CHOICES

Helping our children find humor beyond the forbidden is
clearly a challenge for parents. There is more to humor than
capitalizing on discomfort and it's our job to pass on to our
children how to do that. As in all aspects of parenting, information is critical to guiding our children's choices.

**The more we preview television programs, movies, and
web sites ourselves, the better we will be able to evaluate
whether they use constructive or destructive humor to produce laughter.** I know parents who patrol TV channels for
offensive programming but abdicate the Internet to their children because the parents are intimidated by computers. Staying
current with technology and the information accessed by your
children across all technological breakthroughs may be daunting, but it is important. Some humor web pages actually rate

their humor material using the conventional movie ratings of X, R, PG, and G. However, as with movie ratings, these evaluations are often dependent upon the maturity of the person making the rating.

While we benefit from increasing exposure to positive humor, it can be equally beneficial to be exposed to destructive humor as well. Radio programs such as Garrison Keillor's, *A Prairie Home Companion,* on the Public Broadcasting Network, or those by comedians like Sinbad, who lean toward family-oriented humor are full of positive humor experiences. A friend of mine accidently happened upon humor that was not slanted for his children's consumption. He attended a work-sponsored family party where a comedian used humor that was inappropriate for the youngsters in the audience. He told me that he had the choice of leaving, as many parents did, or remaining and seizing the opportunity to discuss his 9- and 10-year-olds' reactions to the experience. Leaving would have removed the children's exposure to negative humor, but it would not have offered the opportunity for meaningful discussion.

A willingness to expose yourself to the humor tastes of your adolescent and suspend judgment in lieu of gaining an understanding of its appeal to your teenager at least sets the foundation for dialogue. If you have not intervened in the early development of your child's humor tastes, and if you are faced with teenagers whose humor perspective falls outside your control and sensibilities, you will have to work from wherever those humor tastes are now. Many parents discount their adolescents' humor as "sick and disgusting." Making a judgment without trying to appreciate the enjoyment your teenager derives from the humor makes you an outsider and decreases your ability to influence his or her future humor choices.

I had a friend whose preadolescent would make joking, sarcastic remarks and sounds in the voices and mannerisms of the cartoon characters Beavis and Butthead. Upon determining the origin of this unacceptable behavior, the father banned the behavior and the show from the house. Despite this ban, however, the behavior persisted. Finally, the father suggested that they watch the show together. After recovering from the initial shock, the son agreed to sit down with his father for an hour-long viewing of the program. Rather than be automatically critical of the tone and emphasis of the program, my friend asked his son questions concerning aspects of the program the son enjoyed, and my friend was able to point out some of the parodies he thought were clever. Later the conversation shifted to concerns that each of them had about the show. After the discussion, the father lifted his ban on the program, and the preteen took greater responsibility for viewing the program and for his behavior that had been associated with it. The program and its influence in the household were no longer noted. Afterward, my friend felt a private victory when his son demonstrated no interest in seeing the feature-length movie based on the characters from the television show.

As children age, control gives way to influence.
Such influence is based on a mutually respectful relationship
and open exchange of ideas—even about what makes things funny.

As with so many other aspects of parenting, it becomes important to focus on teaching and demonstrating constructive humor early in your child's life. If you have not related to your child from a perspective of humor beginning in his early childhood, your foundation for using it effectively with him as an adolescent may be a bit shaky. But it's never too late to start.

Adolescents are volatile. In the same breath they can yell that they hate you and wish they had never been born unto you and ask you to drive them to the mall. Seeing the humor in the erratic behavior of a hormonally charged adolescent can help you put them in perspective. This perspective shift, in turn, represents an important survival skill—for you as well as for them.

Open the Door and Let Humor In

16 ACTIVITY SIXTEEN ....
Role Play

Watch a TV program together that you suspect may have what you consider inappropriate use of humor. After the program is over:

1. Ask your child to role play you and, as you, discuss what was good about the program and what was not.
2. Now it's your turn. You, as your child, tell what you believe was positive about the program and what was not.
3. Did you agree? If not, what were the differences?
4. Did you judge one another's opinions or simply share them?
5. Did you have fun? What was the outcome of your discussion?

17 ACTIVITY SEVENTEEN ....
Joke-Jitsu

Set up a family night in which you come up with effective joke-jitsu strategies. Use the examples in this chapter to start you off. Provide a few examples for your family. Then, have everyone create some spontaneously—no holds barred.

18 ACTIVITY EIGHTEEN ....
Creative Family Histories

Materials needed: Paper, writing utensil or a tape recorder

When Nora was younger she would occasionally look at her siblings and say, "I must have been adopted." Actually she would chant it over and over, hoping to make it true. Your family can recreate its history. You can go back as many generations as you like. Do this collectively as a group, or have each individual write (or tape) their own history and then share it with the group.

Here's your chance to playfully make up your own explanation of differences between family members, such as how Bill really got those green eyes, or how Sue is the tallest in the bunch. It can be a great format for examining differences between family members in a nonthreatening way. Each person can explore family quirks and offer his or her version of the real story.

CHAPTER SEVEN

The PAYOFF of DIVERGENT THINKING

"Laughter is the shortest distance between two people."
—VICTOR BORGE

A S YOU ARE ALREADY AWARE, the things that make us laugh tend to change as we grow older. Humor can play an important role in the formation of the thoughts that lead to creativity.

Divergent thinking is the process of providing new and unique responses to problems or situations. This thought process is in direct contrast to convergent thinking, which is the process of zeroing in on the "most correct" answer.

Let's use a comb as an example. We use convergent thought to determine the *most common use* of the comb. We use divergent thinking skills to face the challenge of listing *all possible uses* of a comb.

Children who have strong creative skills rate high in humor appreciation. The reason for this is probably that humor and creativity both draw on divergent thinking. Humor skills help children develop an aptitude for understanding and dealing with the unexpected—a skill highly prized in the martial arts and one we can all value in our day-to-day challenges.

MAKE-BELIEVE AND FANTASY

Preschoolers primarily find humor during play. They derive pleasure from "acting funny." Their laughter is most likely to emerge from imagination, fantasy, and make-believe and is minimally dependent upon their verbal skills. Preschool children learn about reality through their experiences in fantasy. They understand the boundaries of the real world and are amused by the ways they can create the impossible or unexpected through make believe.

Jerome and Dorothy Singer,[10] pioneer researchers in the area of children's use of make-believe, have suggested that encouraging a child's experience of make-believe and fantasy is essential for brain activity and stimulation. College students who are very creative report having daydreamed and having had more imaginary companions in childhood than their less-creative cohorts. In essence, the encouragement of fantasy and make-believe enhances laughter for the preschooler and helps intensify the divergent thinking processes critical to creative intelligence.

As children play, they manipulate objects and ideas and expand their knowledge of the world. They create unique and novel situations that expand their understanding of how the world works.

Preschoolers laugh when things don't fit with their usual experiences. They laugh when a parent pretends to be a dog that says "meow." The awareness that dogs bark causes the child to be amused by the unexpected and make-believe sound being produced by the parent.

Fiona marvels at my reaction when she says, "Daddy work." She frequently tells Nora that "Daddy work" when I am not in the house. She has the idea that when I am not home, I am likely at work. When I am with her, but not paying attention, she will come up to me and say, "Daddy work" and begin to laugh. Fiona's laughter reflects her awareness that she is diverging from reality in a playful way. The phrase "Daddy work" makes me laugh and pick her up while saying, "Daddy is not at work. Daddy is home." She usually continues this game by saying, "No. Daddy work." She knows she's got me on this one. The cycle continues until one of us gets bored.

Parents of preschoolers can provoke laughter in their children through simple make-believe play that demonstrates exaggerated or unexpected deviations. Also parents can playfully manipulate certain aspects of concepts understood by the child—for example, a talking lamp or a singing flower. Such manipulation also causes pathways in their brains to be activated, exercising and strengthening their divergent thinking skills.

ENGAGING INCONGRUITIES OF WORDPLAY HUMOR

Children become more focused on language when they are in the first and second grades. The world of words opens to them as their reading and writing skills emerge. Their developmental challenge is no longer limited to understanding basic properties and concepts about the real world. In the early school years, children are pressed to understand the rules involved in constructing words (phonics) and the principles of arranging words to form ideas (grammar and syntax). As they explore words and the rules associated with them, they find many engaging incongruities. Naturally, unexpected properties of words serve as the basis for much of the wordplay humor experienced in the early grade school years. Parents also find themselves enjoying their children's unexpected violations of thought or word usage.

A friend's son was talking about his sister's inability to tolerate milk and, mishearing the word *lactose,* said she had a "toast intolerance." Another wanted to know if Hamlet was a little pig and why the three wise men brought Jesus frankfurters. Surely your children have provided their share of misspoken or misunderstood moments. Savor them—they are gems.

Ambiguity and Incongruity. One of the first things children learn as they become more aware of language is that many words have more than one meaning, or that the meaning of a word is ambiguous when you hear it. If a word can mean two different things depending upon the way it is used, intentionally injecting the wrong meaning into a situation can be funny. This type of humor is often referred to as "word-meaning ambiguity." Here's an example:

Q UESTION:
How do you stop a charging rhino?
A NSWER:
You take away his credit cards.

This joke exploits the fact that, to a child, the word "charging" most commonly means that a rhinoceros is attacking. It is through the double meaning of the word *charging*—and the unlikelihood that a rhino would be in possession of a credit card—that a child finds humor in the joke.

Two words can sound the same but have different meanings. The similarity of sounds can be used to misdirect the child's expectations. This misdirection has been termed "phonological incongruity." An example is:

Q UESTION:
What has four wheels and flies?
A NSWER:
A garbage truck.

The pun is on the word *flies* meaning insects as opposed to meaning fly away.

Puns and Riddles. A pun is often defined as a short quip followed by a long groan. Exploitation of the ambiguity of words is commonly thought of as making puns. Puns are frequently used as vehicles in children's riddles. When children laugh at a pun, they are demonstrating pleasure with their ability to understand the unexpected meaning. A simple riddle involves a one-sentence question with the pun imbedded in it. For example:

Q UESTION:
What is black and white and read all over?
A NSWER:
A newspaper.

The pun is on the words *read* and *red,* which sound exactly alike when spoken.

Interest in riddles continues until approximately age 10 for most children. The complexity of riddles and children's jokes usually increases with the age of the child. For children up through age 10, humor usually takes a question and answer format but relies on qualities of language other than similar sounding words or words with double meaning.

For example, humor can be derived from violating rules of grammar and syntax, as in the following example:

QUESTION:
What animal can jump as high as a tree?
ANSWER:
All animals. Trees can't jump.

By age 10, children tend to respond to humor that looks at relationships between objects or takes the form of jokes more common to adult humor. A variety of increasingly complex strategies are used in humor as children mature.

Imbedded Words. This form of humor is demonstrated by finding words imbedded in other words. For example:

QUESTION:
What kind of key is difficult to turn?
ANSWER:
A donkey.

QUESTION:
What room can no one enter?
ANSWER:
A mushroom.

The Setup. Children's humor frequently works by getting them to form a false assumption. This technique is called the setup.

Setup: *Four friends walked to school under one umbrella. Why didn't they get wet?*
Answer:
It wasn't raining.

Setup: *Name three things that contain milk other than butter and cheese.*
Answer:
Ice cream, cows, and goats.

Similarly, if the child is expecting a humorous punch line, humor can arise by an unexpectedly logical response. For instance:

Question: *If you drop a white dress in the Black Sea, what does it become?*
Answer:
Wet.

Question:
What kind of people usually go to heaven?
Answer:
Dead people.

Confusing Relationships. Often a riddle's question will cause children to make associations that are not commonly drawn. For example:

Question:
What question can never be answered with a yes?
Answer:
Are you sleeping?

Q UESTION:
  What's yours but used more by others than by you?
A NSWER:
  Your name.

Similarities and Differences. In school, children are frequently asked to compare and contrast many different ideas. Such similarities and differences appear in riddles such as:

Q UESTION:
  How are a boy with a cold and a wise boxer alike?
A NSWER:
  One blows his nose, while the other knows his blows.

Q UESTION:
  What's the difference between a flea and a dog?
A NSWER:
  A dog can have fleas but a flea cannot have dogs.

Sniglet Development. Comedian Rich Hall was the first to create sniglets. *Sniglets* are words that should appear in a dictionary but don't. They reflect experiences or situations that are yet to be named. Sniglets force parts of commonly used words together to describe new concepts. One of my friends explores divergent thinking by forming sniglets with her children. Here are some results of their sniglet efforts:

PHONESIA. The affliction of dialing a phone number and, just as your party answers, forgetting whom you were calling.

ELECELLERATION. The mistaken notion that the more you press an elevator button, the faster it will arrive.

Cartoon Captions. Understanding cartoons requires an awareness of the unexpected events or comments often experienced by the characters in them. You can aid your children's development of novel responses to such cartoons by erasing the words in the captions and allowing your children to generate their own novel and frequently funny comments. Invisions, Inc. has developed a game based on completing cartoon captions called "Gagline: The Unique Cartoon Caption Game."[11] In the game, players compete to create the funniest captions to captionless cartoons. The cartoons are later used as story starters for further divergent thinking.

Funny Endings to Familiar Phrases. Dreaming up novel and funny endings to familiar phrases can strengthen divergent thinking in your child. Children resist the urge to respond with expected responses and are encouraged instead to produce unique answers.

Some gems from children I've worked with include:

Don't count your chickens—
until you've closed the door to their coop.

Don't bite the hand—
of someone who doesn't wash after using the toilet.

If at first you don't succeed—
hire someone to do it for you.

You can lead a horse to water but—
you can't lead water to a horse.

Comparing Unrelated Items. We can make up riddles for which we don't have answers as a test for our ability to form novel relationships between objects. In their book, *If They Are Laughing, They're Not Killing Each Other,* Cheryl Miller Thurston and Elaine Lundberg[12] give an example of how this technique can work in the classroom.

One teacher decided to test this idea by asking her students to answer a question to which she couldn't think of a single answer: "How is a jar of peanut butter like a train? In just a few moments, a student raised her hand and said, "They both have a choo (chew)." The teacher decided to ask more questions that she couldn't answer, and she was almost always surprised by how inventive her students could be when they were not searching for one right answer.

THE GIFT OF FLEXIBILITY

Debates are ongoing regarding whether divergent thinking is genetically determined or the result of a child's learning experiences. While a child's outside experiences can determine a great deal of what he learns, a child's environment appears to be most critical to divergent thought. As parents we have a great deal of impact on the development of divergent thought in our children, even if we are not divergent thinkers by nature.

When asked by a teacher, "What is 10 X 20?" an amusing divergent response might be, "If you can't answer that, you shouldn't be teaching the class." However, this kind of genius is not necessarily appreciated by most teachers.

Since conformity is central to the school experience, convergent thinking is traditionally emphasized there, but we can always offer divergent thinking exercises at home.

The importance of divergent thought becomes apparent when we examine "gifted and talented students." By definition these children demonstrate outstanding potential in intellect, creativity, an academic area, or leadership. Research on these students has shown that they possess many shared characteristics that are consistent with having an advanced sense of humor. Most noted among these is flexibility of thought, a trait likely to help any child through life's changes and challenges.

Children who use humor readily tend to:

* *master language more readily,*
* *cope with change more easily,*
* *envision uncommon relationships more clearly,*
* *solve problems more creatively,*
* *take more reasonable risks, and*
* *develop cognitive skills that go beyond those typically strengthened in the classroom.*

All children are gifted—each in his or her own way. Humor is a tool that can enhance children's intellectual development and expand their overall flexibility in dealing with problems that come before them. If only it could help them clean their rooms.

THE PAYOFF OF DIVERGENT THINKING

Open the Door and Let Humor In

19 ACTIVITY NINETEEN ....
Say What?

Materials needed: Two or more people

Here's a fun game our cousins Ryan and Chelsea play that can help develop divergent thinking. Make up a silly sentence, i.e., "For breakfast I had turnips with top hats." Your conversational partner would then say something like, "For lunch I had a peanut butter sandwich in an overcoat." You would then say something equally ridiculous: "For dinner I had steak with smelly sweat socks and sneakers on," and so on.

Does it sound silly? You bet it does. With a little practice, you will be amazed at how your creativity will stretch and your silliness quotient will break new barriers.

20 ACTIVITY TWENTY ....
Congruent Thinking: Blast from the Glass

Materials needed: Cheap plastic or discarded eyeglasses, paper, glue, markers, leftover fabric, and other "craft" items.

Create silly glasses that you can wear when things get a little too heavy around the house. Take cheap plastic glasses or old discards from garage sales. Add any decoration you choose, but make them reflect you and your unique character. Create the kind of glasses a congruent thinker would wear. Create glasses for a divergent thinker. The point is not to make one wrong and one right, but merely to enjoy and laugh about the differences.

Perhaps you could try gumballs attached to pieces of wire dangling over the lenses, or whirlpool shapes drawn onto circles of paper and placed in the frames. Your comic vision might be enhanced by placing huge purple and orange eyebrows of fabric or fake fur on the tops of the frames. Maybe ice cream cones with holes cut out of the bottom, glued to the front of the frames is more your style.

These glasses should signal to everyone that you simply need a little space to get in touch with your humor vision. Each member of the family can be encouraged to use them when their sight becomes clouded with the overly serious.

21 ACTIVITY TWENTY-ONE ....
Family Comic Strips

Materials needed: Children's coloring books, family pictures or comic section from the paper, crayons, pencils

Take children's coloring books or cartoons—be sure to choose your own and your child's favorites—and rip out single pages. Color the pictures and write your own captions. You can also take cartoons from the newspaper, white out their captions, and invite family members to create their own. To truly personalize this activity, use family pictures, either singly or in sequence, and create captions or stories for them.

CHAPTER EIGHT

PUTTING THINGS in PERSPECTIVE

"After God created the world,
He made man and woman.
Then, to keep the whole thing from collapsing,
He invented humor."
—MARK MCGINNIS

I WAS TALKING with an eight-year-old client about the conflict he was having with his sister. "She just keeps bugging me," he said. "It's like she lives to torture me." After I thought the issue was resolved, he asked, "Do I have to love my sister?" He was hoping that God's love and the love of their parents would be enough for her.

Some days it's difficult to get along with the forces of the universe, whether they are little sisters, bosses, spouses, or our own children. Occasionally, I wake up and the sun streams in gently through my window. The birds sing softly. I bound from bed with inexhaustible energy. I look in the mirror and say, "Joseph, you are the master of your destiny."

All right, so those days are extremely rare; even when they do occur, things change quickly. Fiona begins to cry, Andrew wakes up and my tranquillity is shattered. That's when I remember that I am not in control of the world around me. On the days when I watch the evening news, this awareness comes as quite a relief.

*I recognize that the universe has made plans
without consulting me first.
I understand that I don't control the events in my life—
only my reactions to them.*

Thank heaven, I am seeing the light more and more. The only person in this world I can control is myself—and even him I have trouble with. The more we participate in the self-deceit that we are in control, the more dissatisfied we are as parents or as people, for that matter. These are the times we need to put things in perspective.

Using humor at these times puts us at peace with our sense of powerlessness. It helps us develop rapport and encourages cooperation with our children. Ask yourself:

Do I really want to control my child?
                          -or-
Do I want to be a person my child wants to spend time with?

Do I want to be able to just tell my kid what to do?
                          -or-
Do I want to be a parent who helps my kid learn to know what to do?

*Parenting is not about your child submitting her will to you
but about her willingness to be influenced by you.*

Humor and play serve to motivate, educate, and forge the relationship from which influence flows. A child confessed to me, "I don't listen to my dad. He doesn't pay attention to me. Until he starts listening, I'm on strike."

Scolding your children for not obeying or not acting in a way you deem appropriate sends a message that you do not understand who they are. Maybe you don't. Maybe they deserve the scolding. Nevertheless, disciplining your children in a firm but nonthreatening way keeps the door open. They listen; they feel listened to; they feel that you are on their side. When you add laughter and play, you send the message that although this matter may be grave, and we may need to continue discussing the problem, it's possible to put the situation in perspective:

> ♣ *Let's understand that it's not acceptable to hurt or disrespect other people.*
> ♣ *Let's get calm and honor one another's point of view.*
> ♣ *Then, let's laugh together at the crazy things we humans do.*

INCREASING POSITIVE INTERACTIONS

All relationships benefit from fun and emotionally positive experiences. Success in marriage, for example, depends largely on the frequency of positive interactions. In other words, you're more likely to sustain a healthy relationship if you add two happy experiences than if you try to take away two negative ones. The way to make this work? Start creating positive exchanges. The theory is simple: People tend to reciprocate the behavior they receive.

Even though happy couples exchange many negative interactions, it is the ratio of positives to negatives that matters most. So, even if you maintain the number of negative interactions in a relationship but increase the number of positive ones, your chances for success in that relationship increase.

As parents, much of what we do with our children could be considered negative interaction. "Mom, can I watch more TV?" "Dad, can Jason spend the night?" "Can I stay out an hour later with the car?"

In many of these situations you have to say "no," unless of course you allow your children to have free rein with your money, material goods, time, and household order. Overly permissive parenting doesn't work and, in fact, has proven to be destructive. A child constantly searches for limits, and if no one provides them, he keeps searching and testing.

*It is the job of children
to explore the limits of the world around them.
By facing and respecting the limits they encounter every day,
they are challenged to survive into adulthood.*

The point is to create limits in a positive way. My favorite way, of course, is by sharing more humor. Our children must learn that there is a limit to the amount of sun to which the human body can be exposed. There is a limit to the amount of cotton candy a person can consume at one sitting. And there are limits to childrens' behavior in the social world. If they do not learn the limits of the natural world, they are at risk for not being able to physically survive. If they are not able to learn social limits, they may start to believe they deserve social benefits they haven't earned, or they may believe that limits, rules, and laws that apply to others do not apply to them. Parents who are conflicted about enforcing the rules of social behavior often rob their children of clarity and security concerning expectations and limits. But all of this can be taught and provided creatively—with compassion, humor, and play.

ELIMINATING THE NEGATIVE SPIRAL

Andrew frequently wants me to read him "one more book" prior to bedtime. Having established the number that would be read in advance, I say "no," which normally prompts him to ask, "Why not?"

On sane evenings, when I am not interested in increasing the negative interaction between us, I will just laugh and say, "Good night, Andrew." Often he will laugh, too, and go quietly into the night. Other evenings, when I am willing to dance in the land of the negative, I actually answer his question. As an adult male of average intelligence, I know that a five-year-old boy who is trying to extend his bedtime really doesn't want his question answered.

When I do answer, however, I normally appeal to one of three themes:

❖ *"We discussed this before we started."*
❖ *"It's late."*
❖ *"I'm the parent, and I said so."*

Andrew has his standard responses to each of the themes, which include:

❖ *"It can be negotiated."*
❖ *"It's not too late for just one more."*
❖ *"I wish I had the kind of parent who would read me one more book."*

He's very young, but somehow he knows that last one is a real zinger. The implication is, naturally, that I am not a good parent unless I read him one more book. We continue to banter back and forth for as long as I am willing to be engaged. This is often longer than it would have taken to read another book in the first place and certainly longer than it would have taken for me to kiss him, shut out the light, and leave.

We can eliminate the negative spiral that occurs after a limit has been set—most often with humor. I have made a list and numbered Andrew's most common reasons for not going to sleep. Similarly, I have listed and numbered my most common responses. Andrew has memorized his list and its corresponding number. These days, after I finish his last book, Andrew says, "Four." This means, he needs a snack, to which I say, "Three," which means, "You should have gotten it earlier." For the time being, our numbers game is decreasing the nightly bedtime drama and we're having fun doing it.

Humor, laughter, and play allow us to say yes to our children without compromising limits. "Yes, we will take the time together to play on the monkey bars." "Yes, I will wear the clown wig." "Yes, I will listen to your riddle" (no matter how silly it might be). "Yes, I will listen to the new compact disc of the Dead Zombies."

GETTING TO THE SAME SIDE

I may be going out on a limb here, but although you may think the following statement reflects an unrealistic psychological theory, I believe it to be true: Parents and children are on the same side.

You may want to read that again to give the incredulity a chance to wear off. There certainly have been moments when Nora and I have circled the wagons as we retreated to safety, but when I look at the big picture, I perceive my statement to be accurate.

When Fiona will not stop demonstrating her lung capacity in a restaurant, and Nora and I have to experience our meal from the scenic confines of the car, I see her as an adversary. When Andrew becomes increasingly restless or unruly in church and I forgo the pastor's message for a walk around the building, I see my son as the enemy. But my job as parent is bigger.

It is not my job as parent to control my child.
It is my duty to develop a relationship
that encourages my child to understand self-control.

Here are some questions to ask yourself when you find yourself caught in the web of antagonism:

1. Am I seeing my child as an adversary?
2. What's the situation that's helping me dwell in that perception?
3. Do I want to control him/her right now?
4. If I really could, how would I begin to control him/her?
5. Who is the only person I can control?
6. In control of myself, what can I do to help my child learn self-control?
7. What can I do to enhance the relationship between my child and me?

The first step in making certain that you and your child are on the same side is to recognize that when you see your child as an adversary, you are undoubtedly operating from the mistaken belief that you need to control her. Letting go of control, putting her on the same side of the fence you are on, and figuring out what the two of you can do together will help you find a solution. Put down your swords and join together in your conflict.

The relationship between my child and me is of far greater importance than the behavioral problem du jour. If I am able to maintain a rapport with my children and be of influence, I have the ability to help them make sound decisions. If they perceive me to be authentic, consistent, playful, and slow to judge, the conflicts we endure will promote learning and a greater ability for them run their lives in my absence. And none of this has anything to do with being lenient. I can be genuine, constant, mischievous, and nonjudgmental, and still provide my children with lessons to learn. If, however, I am rigid, overly judgmental, and in need of control, I rob them of their ability to gain a sense of mastery over their own environment.

Open the Door and Let Humor In

22 ACTIVITY TWENTY-TWO ....
Increase Positive Interactions

Hang a Chalkboard

Hang a chalkboard in a common family area, such as the kitchen. Every time someone invokes a positive interaction, chalk it up on the board. See how many positive interactions you can chalk up in a day.

Take a Vote

Arrange a family night in which every family member is responsible for suggesting one positive interaction that he or she would like everyone in the family to practice.

Take a vote. Let each member vote for his or her favorite positive interaction. Whichever gets the most votes wins. Those who "lose" are challenged to keep the interaction positive.

23 ACTIVITY TWENTY-THREE ....
Something Funny Happened!

Write it down. Tape-record it. Keep track of it—in an album, notebook, or file. Pull it out when everyone's frustrated, depressed, and needs to laugh. Or save it for holidays when everyone can sit around and enjoy the collection.

24 ACTIVITY TWENTY-FOUR ....
Getting to the Same Side

Arrange for a meeting between the adversaries in your family. Ask them:

1. *Are you seeing this person as an adversary?*
2. *What's the situation creating that perception?*
3. *Do you want to control him/her right now?*
4. *In reality, who is the only person you can control?*
5. *What can you do to help this person learn self-control?*
6. *What can you do to enhance the relationship between you?*

CHAPTER NINE

BEING THERE

"Life itself cannot give you joy unless you really will it.
Life just gives you time and space. It's up to you to fill it."
—CHINESE PROVERB

I HAVE A FRIEND who was inconsolable after the death of his father. He was angered by the fact that he was just getting to know the man who had been inaccessible to him during his childhood. Initially he expressed little anger over the lost years because his "father had to work." At a deeper level, however, he resented the fact that they had never connected when he was younger. Like so many of us who play the "my life could have been better if" game, he felt that his teen years would have run more smoothly had his father been available.

For six months before his father's heart attack they actually talked as they visited mountain streams and golf courses. At last, after his father's retirement they were finally making up for missed opportunities. After his father died, my friend's sadness was compounded by the awareness that he and his father always could have been close if they had only had the chance.

His story is lamented almost exactly in the song, "Cat's in the Cradle" by Harry F. Chapin and Sandra Campbell Chapin:

The cat's in the cradle and the silver spoon,
Little boy blue and the man in the moon,
When you coming home, Dad?

I don't know when,
But we'll get together then, son,
You know we'll have a good time then.[13]

MAKING TIME AND AFFORDING OPPORTUNITIES

To have a good time with our children we need to afford them opportunity. Despite the fact that most of us acknowledge that our families are our priority, financial and social realities make life complicated. Recent research suggests that in the last 25 years the number of hours Americans work has increased by approximately 20 percent, from 40 hours per week to over 48 hours per week. At the same time, leisure time has decreased for the average person by about 30 percent. As work time increases, family time becomes harder to find.

Along with modifications in work patterns have come changes in the family itself. In the past 40 years we have witnessed the breakdown of the extended family, increased divorce rates, and a rise in single-parent households.

In 1992 only about 10 percent of all American households represented the "ideal" home, in which there are two parents and one wage earner. The complicated and exhausting job of providing a household, maintaining it, and addressing the needs of children today is often carried out by one person, in contrast to the not-so-distant past, when several generations of adults in the same household shared child-rearing duties. Single parents often find themselves emotionally and physically exhausted by the time the workday, household chores, dinner, and homework are completed. Quality time with their children becomes something akin to the last mile of a marathon. One working mother said, "I don't have time to worry about parenting. It's something that happens—on the way to the store, soccer practice, and dance lessons."

Even two-parent households are more likely to have both adults in the workforce. Before 1940, young, single women were the only females likely to be employed. Over the next 30 years women worked outside of the home in growing numbers, and by 1970 it was common for women with school-aged children to have a job away from home. Recent trends have shown increased employment for mothers of preschool children and babies. Juggling the demands of work, home, and marriage often diminishes the ability of both parents to engage in activities with their children. Home life can often be reduced to a race for completion of household duties before parents run out of energy.

Due to their hectic pace, parents often don't have time to get the social support they need. These parents often lack the time to nurture relationships and friendships that could provide them a brief respite from parenting demands.

SCHEDULING IS THE KEY

Many of us are experiencing our entire lives "along the way." The problem is we aren't sure which way we are going. The life simplification movement going on quietly in America seems to suggest that many of us are trying to plan our destinations. Examination of our lives often uncovers a clutter of pointless activities and a confusion between wants and needs. More people seem to be reviewing their priorities with regard to their families. They are asking themselves:

+ *What are my priorities?*
+ *What lifestyle choices have I made that are consistent with my priorities?*
+ *What choices have I made that are not consistent with my family?*
+ *What short-term and long-term goals can I make to bring my life in line with family priorities?*
+ *How will I measure progress toward my goals?*

Living a life consistent with our stated priorities is likely to bring about a clearer sense of purpose in family life and greater overall happiness. Mahatma Gandhi said it well:

"Happiness is when what you think, what you say,
and what you do are in harmony."

Finding time is difficult for all of us, but if we wait for time to present itself in order to be with our children, it will never happen. I have a six-page list of things I plan to do when I find the time. Despite my apparently busy schedule, I have noticed that I find the time to meet my employer's needs. Can't I use the same ingenuity to schedule times around my children's needs?

I was appalled to learn that only 50 percent of Americans still sit down together every night at the dinner table—and even those that do are together less than thirty minutes. And I know that I am among the other 50 percent. I frequently leave home before my children are awake and return after they have had dinner. How, you well might ask, do I have time to write a book? The answer is— The book was ghostwritten by Andrew and Fiona—true prodigies.

In an effort to connect with my son, I have scheduled "guy time." These are moments when I lie near him in his bed, and we talk about the significant and silly events of his day. We laugh, joke, sing, read, make-believe, wordplay, and throw all caution to the winds. During "guy time," Andrew and I often talk about the Sunday afternoon off-road adventures his grandfather and I took. Fiona frequently receives honorary "guy time" these days, now that she's getting older. I guess we can't call it "guy time" when I'm playing with Fiona. I'll ask her what she thinks. Maybe she'll want to make up her own name for our time together.

Just as a boss might require a satisfactory explanation of lost work time, Andrew demands an explanation if "guy time" doesn't happen. I dread explaining to him why his time was sacrificed, and I miss the pleasure of being with him. In his world, few things can justify my absence. "Guy time" works for Andrew and me. It is a time that we know is exclusively ours. Only you and your family members can find ways to share the time you need with one another, but scheduling is the key.

In addition to those play periods that occur spontaneously, you must set aside specific times to play with your children.

THE LOW COST AND HIGH CONTACT OF PLAY

Look at your present schedule.

❧ *Where can you make more play or interactive time available with your children?*
❧ *How can you develop a ritual around this time?*
❧ *What will you need to do to make sure that other time pressures don't encroach?*

How you find the time to show up is not important. Making the time is what counts. It may be during the tumble-dry cycle, in the middle of meal preparation, or a late night giggle session on the floor.

Nora and I have recently embarked on once-a-week "family home evenings" where we do craft projects together, read stories, and discuss social values. For example, we read the "King and His Hawk" from William Bennett's *The Children's Book of Virtues*[14] and discussed its moral lesson—the importance of not acting hastily when angered. We also made crowns from beads glued onto gold construction paper so we could all take turns being king. In the past, family home evenings have included the construction of a storybook using family pictures and painting our faces to look like clowns. All such evenings are low cost and high contact. Consider doing the activities outlined at the end of each chapter in this book, or, make up your own.

However it happens, being available to each other is integral to the development of children and parents alike. Making the time and forming a ritual are important, not only to your current relationship with your children but to their memory of you and to their future relationship with their own children.

Doing Is Letting Go of Guilt

There will be times when you simply cannot be there for your children. I don't know how to emphasize this enough, but it is essential to not hold on to those times, so that they do not get in the way of the times you are there. Holding on to things you wish you had done does not benefit you as much as simply increasing the number of times you do what you wish. Remember, it's those positive experiences that count.

There is a story about two monks that addresses the importance of not holding on and of letting go. The monks, who had taken a vow not to communicate or fraternize with women, came upon a stream. As they walked near the stream, they noticed a woman in obvious distress, stuck in the middle of the water. As the men approached the woman, she sought their assistance in getting to the other side.

The monks began to discuss the situation with one another. "You are not going to touch her, are you?"

"I don't know. We should help her."

After pondering the issue, one monk reached out to her and helped her across the water. Approximately a mile later the other monk said, "I can't believe you touched her."

His counterpart responded, "I did. But I let go of her ten minutes ago. Are you still holding her?"

Doing is letting go. Making the time keeps you from worrying that you are not spending enough time. Even though being physically present with your children may not happen as frequently as you would like, once you have made choices that are in accord with your priorities, it becomes imperative to let go of your guilt. That's the only way to be emotionally present with your children. And there is nothing more "in the moment" than a shared laugh.

Open the Door and Let Humor In

25 ACTIVITY TWENTY-FIVE..
My Life Would Be Better If . . .

This is a fill-in-the-blank game. Take turns with family members saying, "My life would be better if . . . " and then fill in the blank. It's all right to use serious thoughts, but the point of the game is to have fun. The game serves as a way to communicate thoughts and feelings that might otherwise be difficult.

Perhaps family members can play off of each other. For example:

Child: *"My life would be better if . . . I owned drums."*

Parent: *"My life would be better if . . . you owned drums and I owned earplugs."*

26 ACTIVITY TWENTY-SIX...
Pass a Story

Materials needed: Willingness to tell a tall tale

This activity may seem familiar to scouts or campfire aficionados. Gather the family together. One person starts a story. After a few lines of the story, the person stops (mid-sentence is particularly effective) and the next person picks up the story. The object is to come up with the wildest and wackiest story possible. Friends have warned us that this exercise has created so much laughter that several family members were crying. That's one of the beauties of laughter. You get two emotions for the price of one.

27 ACTIVITY TWENTY-SEVEN ....
Pass a Picture

Materials needed: Paper—the longer the better, some type of drawing tool. Absolutely no aptitude for art.

"Pass a Picture" is similar to "Pass a Story." The first artist draws a head, or hair. He hides his artwork, except for the bottom inch or less, by folding it back, or under. The next artist works from the portion she can see and creates the next segment of the body, then folds back the majority of her work. This continues until the figure is completed. The last artist has the honor of unfolding the paper to reveal the masterpiece. Members of small families may need to draw more than one section of the picture. Large families can draw the figures in smaller segments, or create multiple figures standing on each other's shoulders. Imperfections increase the hilarity. Pictures can be of any subject or form. You set the guidelines.

28 ACTIVITY TWENTY-EIGHT ....
Humor Collages

Materials needed: Old magazines, newspapers, photographs, glue, scissors, paper

For those of you who may feel a bit threatened by drawing your own pictures, this project is for you. Cut out a variety of pictures from old magazines, newspapers, or photographs. The pictures need not be funny in themselves. Create a new picture by gluing several of the pictures together. Mismatched heads and body parts particularly get a good guffaw. If you really want to go wild, blend animals, humans, and objects together. The sillier the better. Display your art with pride.

CHAPTER TEN

BREAKING HABITS, SHIFTING ROLES

"Enjoy yourself. These are the good old days
you're going to miss in the years ahead."
—ANONYMOUS

I WAS SIXTEEN YEARS OLD and had just acquired my driver's
license, which got me a summer job at my Uncle Olen's dairy.
I was given the job of taking a dead calf to the dump and was
entrusted with my uncle's prized dump truck. Although I struggled with standard transmissions at the time, I wasn't about to
reveal this to my uncle.

I reached the top of a hill on the way to the dump and
stopped. I was terrified that I might not be able to get the truck
in gear and would roll back into the car behind me. With one
foot on the brake and the other on the clutch, I thrust my braking foot onto the gas pedal as I removed the clutch. The truck
lurched forward and in my rearview mirror, I saw the calf fly
onto the windshield of the car behind me. After pulling the
truck to the side of the road, I ran back to the car and heard the
hysterical screaming of its occupant. I wondered what the flying
calf must have looked like from her perspective.

As I approached the car I fumbled for words and ended up
saying, "Ma'am, I think you have my calf."

The woman frantically responded, "Get it off! Get it off!"

I lifted the calf from her hood, and she began yelling,
"Wipe it off! Wipe it off!" I removed my T-shirt and cleaned

her window. Before I could exchange information with her, she sped away. She must not have wanted to stay and see what else might happen to her.

I returned bare-chested to my uncle's dairy, having disposed of the calf. My uncle inquired about my trip and the absence of my shirt. I did not tell him the truth. I was afraid that he would never trust me to drive for him again. As I look back now, I believe that he would have understood my humanness, in fact, given his sense of humor, he probably would have gotten a good laugh out of it. But I couldn't admit my weakness to any-one—something that I'm likely to have learned from my family.

As parents, we not only fear admitting our weaknesses
to ourselves, but even more so to our children.

A six-year-old client told me that he didn't deserve his mom, because he isn't as good as she is. He was unable to find any faults in her and didn't believe that when she was a child she had made any of the mistakes he did. Many of us fear letting our children see us as we really are, afraid that if they know "the truth," they will never trust us to care for them; therefore, we must appear to be superhuman. That, after all, is how our parents appeared to us.

FROM CUSTODIAN TO PARENT

A friend of mine used to come home after a long day and rush from the dinner table to read the newspaper. For me this would be a form of torture. Who wants to digest that much dis-aster on a full stomach? Yet, his children knew that when Dad read the paper, it was time to leave him alone.

One evening during the newspaper hour, Sarah, age 7, felt a strong desire to show her father a new Barbie doll her mother had purchased for her that day. Despite several attempts to get his attention, she failed, and began to sigh and whimper as she was leaving the room.

My friend related that he broke free from his paper long enough to appreciate the pain and rejection she was feeling. When he asked her what she needed, she said tearfully, "I just wanted to show you my doll." He set his paper to the side and began to play dolls, like a 7-year-old, with his daughter. Laughter filled the room. Later when he was putting her to bed, he overheard her say excitedly to her sister, "Daddy put the paper down for me."

Do you know people who go to work, not to be productive but to avoid being fired? They are usually people suffering burnout, and I call them R.O.A.D. employees (Retired On Active Duty). Many parents could be described in the same way.

Many parents have lost their ability
to draw meaning from the actions of their children
and simply function as custodians.

Do you think sometimes that's what you are—a custodian of your children? One sign would be that, in the midst of a conversation with your kid, your mind travels to your work, hobbies, the past, or the future, while your body goes through the motions with your children. Sometimes even your body isn't in the game.

A friend told me, joking, "During adolescence, I never saw my father. If he wanted to talk to me, he would yell at me from the living room and I'd yell back from my room."

The other day I was running late for work when Nora said she "needed to take a quick shower." Before I could protest my unexpected and untimely child-watching duty, she slipped away. As I sat with Fiona and Andrew, my mind was full of frustration over my wife's timing, the possible consequences of my being late for work, past parental messages about punctuality, and all potential negative outcomes associated with chronic lateness. In my mind, I was already unemployed, and my family was living under a bridge.

During the course of my internal jumble, Fiona crawled into my lap. Only after her incessant effort to get my attention did I acknowledge her. How can a little person be sitting on you, tugging at you, making every gesture and sound she can, and be so invisible? Finally, I let go of all my self-imposed mind clutter and held her close. In that moment, all that existed was Fiona's warmth against my chest. All my fears had been imagined. All my thoughts were self-manufactured. But this moment was real. The clock didn't matter. The only ticking I heard was the beat of her heart.

I saw an ad on a billboard that read, "My father never misses his tea time." Pictured in it were a set of golf clubs, a father clad in a golf sweater, and his daughter. The dad and daughter were sitting across from one another, sipping tea. It got me thinking that paying attention requires eye-level, direct communication. It occurs on the floor, in tree houses, on swings, in sandboxes, and at tea—on our kids' time schedule, not on ours. When we show up and pay attention, we provide the opportunity to communicate and play.

The pleasure derived from playtime
is critical for difficult times ahead.
The way you interact in play is likely to be
the way you interact in times of trauma.
This is an opportunity you're not going to want to miss.

Many parents play what I call the "When/Then" game. "When I become more financially stable, then I'll have more time to spend with my children," I heard a man say. "When I am under less stress, then I can afford to be more *there* for my son," said a working mother about her 10-year-old.

The child years pass quickly. The sooner you establish your relationship with your children, the more likely long-term benefits will be achieved for all of you. I have worked with dying patients, and you know what? No one goes to his grave complaining that he did not work enough.

FROM PROTECTOR TO NURTURER

This need to hide our own frailties can, without our realizing it, teach our children to seek perfection rather than excellence. This need results from a misunderstanding of our role as parents—a role that changes, requiring us to change with it.

When our children are born,
they rely on us psychologically and physically.
We function as their protectors.
Our strength and their vulnerability shape the relationship.

Fiona was a full-term baby weighing just under seven pounds. I was unprepared for her petiteness. My perception of her helplessness and vulnerability were exaggerated by the fact that she spent the first days of her life strapped to a photoblanket to treat her jaundice. In the first days of her life our entire world centered on helping her get the medical care she needed. We were on danger patrol. It was our responsibility to protect her and nourish her.

With each day, she gained skills and competencies that allowed her greater independence from us. Today, no longer does she require Nora as her food supply, nor does she need me to carry her up or down the stairs. With her broadening abilities, her world expands, and the influences upon her expand as well. Larger than life is not a bad thing for parents to be for an infant. But as Fiona has become more autonomous, which naturally happens during years one to three, she has begun to declare her independence from us. During this time, our role changes from protector to nurturer.

As a nurturer, a parent gratifies
a child's emotional needs via actions, words, and touch.
The focus of care for our children shifts slowly
from their being totally dependent on us
to their developing dependence on themselves.

Learning to let children experience the world on their own with only our counsel and guidance is a difficult transition for many parents. It requires trust that teaching is as important as protection. It involves a willingness to let children learn from pain as opposed to being sheltered from it. Parents who are unwilling to let their children experience life firsthand believe it is their duty as protectors to shelter them at all costs. Unfortunately, with this type of parental interference, children fail to gain knowledge from personal experience, and their options for coping remain restricted. When we as parents can make the transition from protector to guide, we give our children opportunities to learn adaptive skills necessary for the larger battles that loom ahead.

Teaching Excellence Rather than Perfection

It is my primary goal to help you use humor skills in day-to-day parenting, and I believe it is essential for your children to learn these skills from you. The way children deal with human frailties is a determining factor in how they look at life, how they feel about who they are in this life, and whether they believe they are doing their best. Doing one's best is different from trying to be perfect. How children view themselves influences how they respond to life's adversities and temptations.

Taught to focus on perfection, children have less ability to accept their humanity, the flaws, failures, and vulnerable spots that all human beings have. When they are taught to focus on excellence, they are more inclined to endure their weaknesses playfully as opposed to hiding them or seeking to escape them.

When children are taught to seek excellence instead of perfection, they acknowledge their limitations responsibly, without blaming or laughing at others.

As our children attempt to master their environment, they need to see role models who honestly show weakness as well as appropriate ways to cope with it. If we hide our weaknesses from our children behind a parental mask, we fail to nurture them honestly. Instead of saving face by refusing to admit that perhaps you misjudged your child's behavior, what do you think would happen if you were to laugh at yourself? Tell your kid that you hate to admit it, but you acted stupidly and hope she can understand. Perhaps you can imitate yourself being angry.

*Through our ability to laugh at our mistakes
and show our silly side,
we give our children permission to be human as well.*

I worked with a child who convinced me that he did not want to be a "kid" because "kids mess up too much." He perceived childhood as a time of error and adulthood as a time of perfection. His parents described him as a "wonderful young man" and didn't understand why he was having difficulty getting along with other children at school. His view was that all the other children were too immature and prone to getting into trouble. He could not identify another child he was willing to take the risk to get to know. By age eight, he was claiming to live his life by reason rather than emotion. This child needed to discover the joy of being eight before he could ever enjoy being thirty-eight.

Dispensing with Ideal Images

A father told me, "I am deeply invested in looking like what I think a parent should be—which is what my father taught *me* a parent should be. No wonder my adolescent won't admit when he does something wrong. I haven't been much of an example."

Ideal images we carry can get in the way of any relationship and certainly affect the one we have with our children. Being "real" or genuine involves being willing to dispense with judgment of ourselves and others and allowing ourselves to simply be as we are—to show all aspects of ourselves, including our positive, vulnerable, and silly sides. This does not imply that we should do away with values, morals, or standards: Rather, we should teach these lessons gently and playfully. For those who believe they may still have a low silliness quotient, just know that you are never too old to be young.

Effective parents play without worry about maintaining their adult image. They color, play hide-and-seek, and experience the world of make-believe. Since the age of three, Andrew has insisted that we buy Nora toys for her birthday so that she will stop playing with his.

For many of us, playing with a child takes a dramatic change of perspective. I am far more comfortable dealing with healthcare reform, pending financial problems, and increasing college tuition costs than I am making silly faces with my children in public. Effective play requires a willingness to suspend the critical mind and engage the creative muses. The clown wig may be too tight or the music they want to hear too vapid, but who cares? We are there, not as costume designers or music critics, but in the spirit of play.

Learning to enjoy life, not as you want it to be,
but as it is, is essential to effective humor and play.

Favoring Spontaneity over Control

In my clinical practice, I worry about out-of-control children, but I also am concerned about those who are overly controlled. They often appear to be miniature adults, children whose parents are perfectionists and who inadvertently punish and ridicule the childlike qualities out of their youngsters. These children may be well-behaved and submissive, but they often lack the spontaneity and flexibility common among healthy children of similar age. Children who are caged at an early age, fearful of making mistakes, become controlling and less adaptive because they never had the choice.

May your children fail a lot—and as soon as possible.

FROM NURTURER TO ENCOURAGER

As children reach school age, our role as parent changes again. While we still desperately want to protect our kids and nurture them, we find ourselves more in the role of cheerleader or mentor. We function primarily as encouragers of our children's behavior. As our kids become increasingly influenced by their peers, our ability to influence them becomes fragile—able to break at any moment. Since we cannot really control them, our job becomes more that of a coach. We can only do our best to cheer them on when they behave appropriately, forgive them when they do not, and admit to them when we do the same.

In order for us to maintain our influence,
we must maintain our credibility in our children's eyes.
This credibility emerges from a willingness to admit our mistakes,
share our frustrations, and accept responsibility for our errors.

There is a tendency when children reach this stage for parents to want to reassert their control, but the appropriate course of action is just the opposite. Being genuine, open, honest, and responsible with our children allows us to maintain influence in their development.

If I asked you to share your most embarrassing moment, such as my flying calf experience, you would likely tell your story playfully. You might say that the embarrassment was so great at the time you thought you would die. Of course, you did not die. The misery of that moment and the fear of being exposed as real have shifted over time and make a funny story today. I say, save time. Laugh now. You need the laughter more during the crisis than you will later.

Remembering past embarrassment gives us a healthy perspective. It reminds us that we can survive adversity. I encourage families I work with to talk openly about past embarrassments in order to expose weaknesses and to enjoy and delight in one another's imperfections. Confronting our limits in a playful way often liberates us.

Being real means opening ourselves to moments that might otherwise make us uncomfortable. It is beneficial to our souls and to the essence of our children that we get on our play clothes, roll up our sleeves, and run through the house with a squirt gun, dance wildly in our yards, and engage in other activities that most adults fear. By letting go of our preconceived notions of parenting and by saying yes to the spontaneity and love of our children, we, like the Velveteen Rabbit, are made real.

I have people tell me that they wouldn't act like me because it's "stupid" or "silly." These people are confused about the meaning of stupidity and silliness. Stupidity involves lacking knowledge or intelligence. Silliness derives from the old English word *saelig*, which means to be happy and blessed. When I play wildly with my child, I do not feel stupid. I know exactly what I am doing, and in the process of my silliness I am blessed.

It takes a substantial amount of courage to ignore the voices inside our heads that say, "You are too old to be doing this." The reward for your courage, however, is an improved relationship between you and your child. As a result of your bravery, your children learn that *they* take precedence over the worries of adult life.

The silliness of today is the fond memory of tomorrow.
The gifts of being human, equal, real, and vulnerable with your
children are greater than anything you can purchase.

I have a friend who will forever remember the day his father went to school with him dressed like a banana. When they were going home they were stopped by a police officer. As the patrolman cautiously approached the banana-clad driver, the father said, to his son's delight, "I am sorry, officer, if I was going a little fast. I was just getting a little ripe."

When was the last time you let the child within you out to play? What stories will your children tell about you when they are older? What do you want them to remember about you—how hard you worked, or how much fun you were when they were with you?

Open the Door and Let Humor In

29 ACTIVITY TWENTY-NINE ....
A When/Then Letter to My Child

1. If you know you are going to work late this week, write a brief letter to your child (children).
2. In the letter, explain why you cannot come home to play.
3. In the letter, play the When/Then Game. Start a sentence, such as:

When I finish my homework, then _____ .
When I get the house clean, then _____ .
When I've had my milk and cookies, then _____ .

Simply fill in the blank. Create as many "when" phrases as you can. Then, have fun filling them in. The point is to laugh as much as you possibly can.

30 ACTIVITY THIRTY ....
I Love a Picnic

Materials needed: Blanket, silly foods

Picnics are a wonderful way for everyone to relax and let their hair down. Picnics don't have to occur outdoors at your local park. In fact, some of the best picnics we've had have been on the living room floor in the middle of winter. We just put a blanket down in the living room and gather up all of the household plants and set them around. Then we get out the boom box, a little food, and voilá!

Kids love to help. If you add "funny" foods to the mix, such as green eggs and ham or dirt cups (cups of chocolate pudding with crushed chocolate cookies on top and gummy worms all around), it simply gets better.

31 ACTIVITY THIRTY-ONE ....
Different God-Given Strengths

When Andrew was recently teased for swinging a baseball bat "like a girl," and upset about this proclamation, I told him I thought this was a compliment, since his mother has always been a better softball slugger than I am. There was nothing I could do to console him. I merely hugged him, committed to spending more time in batting practice, and announced that we all have different God-given strengths.

One day when I was unsuccessfully attempting to put a bookcase together, I decided to give up and buy a preassembled unit. I told Andrew I would leave the carpentry to people who don't have two left thumbs. He looked at my hands, laughed, hugged me, and said, "That's okay, Dad. We all have different God-given strengths."

1. When was the last time your child showed you his/her personal weakness?
2. When was the last time you showed your child a personal weakness of yours?
3. What can you both learn from this exchange?
4. What can you both laugh about in this exchange?

CHAPTER ELEVEN

ATTENTION to the MOMENT

*"The really happy man is one
who enjoys the scenery on a detour."*
—ANONYMOUS

MUCH HAS BEEN WRITTEN ABOUT the dangers of television viewing. Some have suggested that it makes violence commonplace for children. I believe that nothing is more dangerous about TV than its capacity to distance families through passivity. I speak to parents who admit that they and their kids are "couch potatoes" who enjoy nightly TV watching. They stare aimlessly at the show and do their parenting during commercials. Although there may be enjoyment and even laughter associated with television viewing, it is not conducive to people interacting with one another.

*Brief, direct interaction between family members
produces more laughter than hours of sitting together
watching situation comedies on television.*

Sometimes planning something the whole family can do together seems like work. Perhaps you fear that no one will have anything to say, or that your children will protest so much that you won't have fun. Your willingness to let go of being a grown-up is critical to having fun. Fun, itself, is an invitation for your children to spend more time with you. The more your kids emulate who you are, the more effective a parent you can be.

YOUR POWERS OF FOCUSED THINKING

We live in the age of information. The computer certainly rivals television for our attention. Surfing the net and responding to electronic mail have become alternates to television viewing. Although the computer can be a forum for interaction, as is the case with family-oriented CD ROMs, most experiences with computers are solitary and isolating.

After an overstimulating day, many of us look to the refuge of absorbing, almost numbing, activities like television viewing, catching a video, or getting on-line. These activities can entertain us while not demanding much attention or emotional energy. It's been said by people in other cultures that if you want to drive an American crazy, just put one in a room with white walls and no distractions. The implication is that we have been raised in a civilization where we have difficulty just sitting with our thoughts.

Dr. John Kabat-Zinn teaches "mindfulness meditation"[15] strategies to increase our awareness of each moment. His techniques include training the art of paying attention by placing one raisin in your mouth. By shifting attention from all thoughts and competing sensations, you are to experience all facets of the raisin, as if you had never come in contact with one before. Rather than anticipating the raisin's taste "out of the moment," you languish, with the raisin in your mouth, as you become more aware of the raisin's texture, weight, and temperature "in the moment." It's all a matter of living in the here and now.

Every moment of life, the brain is bombarded by competing inputs. Many of these sensations come from our external world. At this instant you could be paying attention to the feeling of the book against your hand, the hew of the paper, or the contrast of the ink to the background. Other inputs come from our own thoughts. For example, right now you could be thinking about what you're going to be doing during your next vacation, or still thinking about the raisin exercise. Perhaps a child is trying to grab your attention.

We select what stimuli will hold our focus. Most of us have developed patterns of attention that enable our brains to make attention choices easily. For example, the brain determines that you are sitting on the couch looking ahead, and it decides that it should pay primary attention to the television and secondary attention to the family.

Even when we think we are paying attention to our children, often we aren't. In general when human beings communicate, they pay more attention to what they are going to say next than to what the other person is saying right now. Frequently, I find myself saying to Andrew, "Yeah, that's interesting," although my mind has wandered and I didn't hear what he said. Sadly, he is starting to realize that this response means "I was too engrossed in something else to hear you, and I am too stubborn or fearful to admit it."

Often, even when I am listening to Andrew, I don't hear him. In order to reduce the likelihood that my attention will drift to my favorite distractions, I make a conscious effort to decrease the clutter. I turn off the television, sit on the floor with him, and look him in the eyes. And still I will find my mind wandering. Children frequently talk in circles and take longer to get to what adults consider "the point." Slow down. Look. Listen. Be with your child—at his pace.

BEING WITH YOUR CHILD—AT HIS PACE

Honoring the speed of your child's speech style is difficult, but failing to respect it is equal to not respecting his ideas, his world, and—most importantly—his person.

The reward for doing this is that you will enhance your powers of focused thinking. It takes a concentrated effort to give someone your undivided attention. Whether you do it at work, at home, or out in the world, it is an act of respect for others we all can benefit from practicing.

Recently, I have begun to notice the types of thoughts that distract me when I am listening to my children. Since they are mere thoughts, I have a choice regarding when I am going to deal with them. I also have tried to keep a list of mental intrusions and take action to resolve them. The other day, while Andrew was talking, I was thinking about a presentation I needed to prepare for later in the week. I set the thought aside. After we finished talking I completed preparation for that presentation so that when Andrew and I talked the next day, that distraction would not be available.

PROCESS OVER OUTCOME

There is a saying that has helped me uncover a truth about myself—something about how men can go fishing their entire lives and never realize it's not the fish that they are after. For years, I characterized my experience of going fishing based on whether or not I had a full creel of fish when I came home. If there were no fish, there had been no joy in going fishing. Now I enjoy the experience of fishing so much that I can fish in my own bathtub. Of course, I have to be careful with the hooks.

In a broader sense, the saying about fishing has great implications for parenting. We gain a significant parental advantage if we realize that the outcome in any interaction with our children is less important than the process.

The other day Andrew said he had a "headache ache." Wanting to demonstrate my wisdom and to make sure he was properly taught, I corrected him and said, "No. It's a headache." He responded, "Dad, it's my head, and really it's a headache ache."

*Many of the battles we experience with our children
emerge from our need to be right.*

Since very few adults go around saying "headache ache," I am certain that as he matures, he will make the appropriate adjustment. I didn't need to argue with him in that moment and make him wrong, particularly since his headache was aching.

I remember being critical of myself as a young therapist for failing to address an important issue that had been presented to me by a client. My supervisor calmed me considerably, suggesting that the issue would come around again, that such a process is long term, and that there would be ample opportunities. Of course, my supervisor was right.

In the same way, the long-term relationship with our children gives us many chances to get things right. When a situation does not turn out for the best, part of the process is working to understand what caused the outcome; for it is this knowledge that helps us handle the situation properly the next time around. If, for example, your child breaks a toy and then lies about how it got broken, nothing terrible will happen if you don't confront both issues at once. There will be plenty of teachable moments concerning both the importance of taking care of one's things and accepting consequences honestly. I've watched a parent continue to talk to a child until the parent achieved the desired outcome. But you have to ask yourself: What's more important— immediate admission of guilt or time to consider why it's important to be honest? Isn't the manner in which things are handled more important than the specific outcome?

Here's a conversation between Susan and her mother:

Mom: "I want you to say, 'I'm sorry for breaking the lamp.'"
Susan: "I am sorry, Mom."
Mom: "No, I want you to say, 'I am sorry for breaking the lamp.'"
Susan: "I said, I am sorry."
Mom: "I want to hear the words, 'I am sorry for breaking the lamp.'"
Susan: (mockingly) "I am sorry for breaking the lamp."
Mom: "I don't like your tone, young lady. Drop the attitude and say it again."

While it is important to help children experience remorse, in this situation Susan is more likely to come away with a message that has nothing to do with regret. What Susan learns from this conversation is that she had better do things her mother's way. Specific and more important messages about acknowledging responsibility and expressing sorrow are likely to be lost.

> *Over the long haul,*
> *what shapes your child is the process*
> *you use to handle an event.*

Issues of process-versus-outcome happen every day. I am notorious for racing through museums just so I can say I've seen it all. Of course, my out-of-breath family has achieved my goal of "seeing it all" and in the process has experienced nothing. Children, by contrast, can spend so much time involved in the process of life that it can be maddening. Andrew can spend endless hours kicking rocks and jumping into puddles. He usually does not have a goal to kick a certain number of rocks. He simply kicks them because the experience pleases him. When was the last time you did something simply because the experience pleased you?

Whenever we have expectations for our children's behavior during a family outing or any other event, we put ourselves at risk. We all know that outcomes do not always match our hopes. It's like anticipating Christmas. Many adults struggle with this holiday because their hopes, founded in childhood, are simply not attainable. Shifting our focus from an expected outcome of the past to becoming fully engaged in the process of the moment can help put meaning back into an event.

> *The less I try to make an activity turn out the way I want it*
> *and the more I allow myself to be absorbed by the activity,*
> *the more I enjoy it.*

One of the greatest gifts our children offer us is their delight in the simple things of life. Fiona becomes so excited by running down a hallway or playing in the sand. She has no plan for her behavior; it is the behavior itself that she enjoys. I am fascinated by the magic of her joyous attention to the moment. I used to place a lot of structure onto playtime with my kids, setting rules and telling them that play would be more fun if we did it "this way." I realized, however, that I have more than enough chances to tell them how I think they should live their lives. Playtime is not a place for that kind of lesson.

Now during free play, the kids lead. My goal is to have no goals at all during play and to enjoy the journeys they design for me.

APPLYING HUMOR TO UNMET HOPES

Occasionally there will be times when we do have expectations. We simply cannot help ourselves; we are human. When we do, and when those hopes are not met, humor allows us to adapt.

Children frequently bounce off setbacks and spring into other options quickly. I watched a boy attempting to rope a branch on a tree. He was clearly engaged in the process. When the branch was finally captured, he tried to get the rope down with no luck. Rather than becoming disheartened by his rope being stuck, he decided to grab hold of it and swing.

How can you make the most of the road you are on, even if its not the one you've chosen? It's been said that if you want to make God laugh, make plans. We can laugh when our best made plans go awry. It's a decision that we choose to make. The more we find humor in our powerlessness, the more our children will find it as well. So, remember, the next time you're faced with a faltered expectation, grab hold of your rope—and swing.

Open the Door and Let Humor In

32 ACTIVITY THIRTY-TWO ....
Expectations

During a family gathering, have each member write on a piece of paper as many expectations as they conjure up for:

+ *Today*
+ *This week*
+ *Christmas*

Talk about these hopes and expectations, joke about them, and discuss how many of them you think are real, out of the question, possible, outrageous, silly, wonderful, magical, ridiculous.

33 ACTIVITY THIRTY-THREE ....
Creating a Humor-Friendly Environment

I like to think that if you visited our house you would be more impressed with how lived-in and playful it is rather than how clean it is. I have visited homes that look like museums. I always look under the throw rugs for Kool-Aid stains or other indications that the children who live there have roamed free.

Since moving all the adults out of the house is not an option, the following suggestion is offered as a subtle step to increase the humor-friendliness of your home.

FAMILY CANDID CAMERA

Materials needed: Video recorder, tape recorder, or camera; transportation

This activity is one I stole and modified from a story Nora told me about her college days. I'm beginning to wonder just what she did there. Divide your family into two teams. If you live in an area where you can walk to a variety of places and come in contact with various people, no transportation will be necessary. Otherwise you will need to make sure that you have one person per team who can drive or manage the public transit system.

Each team will take their recording device and scour the area for funny happenings or sights. The team will video or audiotape their funny observations. Set a time limit in which teams must come back to base (home.) When the teams have returned everyone share their funny moments. A winning team can be determined by virtue of the laughter they generated. Obviously both teams win by enhancing their awareness of the humor and fun around them.

34 ACTIVITY THIRTY-FOUR ....
Sign, Sign, Everywhere a Sign

Materials needed: Cardboard or poster board, markers or paints

Have you ever had a gaggle of young girls over to the house? The giggling can hit the red zone on the decibel scale. It's a far more pleasing sound than whining, however.

Ever wish you could designate one place where whining or temper tantrums are not allowed? Why not! Create your own unique road signs for the house. One of our favorites is the "No Whining Zone," complete with the picture of a whining child circled and crossed in red.

Here are a few more ideas:

Giggling Area. Proper ear protection required.
Danger! Time-out in progress.
Quiet Please: Frazzled Mother Zone.
Disaster Area. Slap a sign on your teenager's bedroom door when the room needs cleaning, perhaps indicating the date or time when the area hopefully will be safe for human occupancy.

CHAPTER TWELVE

ADJUSTING YOUR COMIC VISION

"From there to here, from here to there,
Funny things are everywhere."
—DR. SEUSS

W HEN NORA WAS PREGNANT, it seemed to me that every woman I saw in the grocery store was pregnant. When I purchased a new car, every car on the road appeared to be not only my model but also my color, and when I peered inside them, the drivers looked a lot like me.

In the same kind of attention shift, opening the door to the joy in our lives and to the freedom of our children's play helps us find even more enthusiasm in our relationship with them. It also helps us become aware of other people who appreciate and attend to joy, too. Happiness begets happiness.

Focusing on joy helps us
recognize the positive interactions
we can have with our kids.

Such an awareness improves our satisfaction in our relationship with our children, which they can sense. As a result, they are more drawn to us, seeking more positive experiences with us. Don't you find that as an adult you are more readily drawn to people who are positive and joyful? Why wouldn't your kids be too?

VARYING YOUR VIEW WITH CARTOON STRIPS AND TELEVISION

Bill Keane's "Family Circus," Lynn Johnson's "For Better or Worse," and Hal Ketchum's "Dennis the Menace" are cartoon strips that frequently deal with parenting issues. These cartoonists present children's behavioral problems, parent's and children's amusing courses of action, and the confusion parents experience. Why not read them together, aloud, and use them as springboards for communication?

I have warned of the dangers of excessive TV watching. As in all things, moderation and discretion are essential. During the times that you elect to watch television, why not plan the form of entertainment you are going to watch together? Which programs will stimulate discussion, fun, learning?

The trials and tribulations of how parents and children relate serve as the source of many humorous cartoons, television programs, and movies. Experiencing this humor may heighten your appreciation of how parenting can be viewed as funny.

Shows like *Father Knows Best, Leave It to Beaver,* and *Mayberry R.F.D.* were very popular many years ago. Some of them are still shown on cable networks. *Family Affair, The Courtship of Eddy's Father, The Brady Bunch, Family Ties, Family Matters,* and *Rosanne* are available through syndication or current programming. Some of the older situation comedies appear to be even more popular now than they were originally.

The volume and success of such programming demonstrates a number of issues:

❧ *Humor in parenting serves a popular function in our society;*
❧ *Despite changes in values over the years, the stress and uncertainty of parenting continue to beg for a humorous perspective; and*
❧ *Changes in the structure of the family pose unique parenting challenges with a variety of potentially humorous situations.*

Programs with themes such as single parenthood (*Grace Under Fire*), dual-income households (*The Cosby Show*), male-directed households and extended family issues (*Full House*) focus on even more diverse situations that are common in today's world.

Some of us deal with our frustrations and tensions associated with family life by watching people in the world of TV struggle with the same frustrations and tension. We admit our confusion and uncertainty through our laughter during these programs and adjust our sense of humor as readily as we adjust the volume.

If you're going to watch television, why not use these programs as vehicles to stir communication and to stay acquainted by laughing together and enjoying one another's company?

FINDING COMEDY IN BOOKS AND MOVIES

Many books address the inherent comedy of being a parent. Some of their authors are celebrities who have become more vocal about their roles as parents—for example, Bill Cosby's *Fatherhood* and *Childhood* and Erma Bombeck's *Motherhood: The Second Oldest Profession* and *Just Wait Until You Have Kids*. Books specific to single parent or working mother humor include *The Working Mother's Guilt Guide: Whatever You're Doing It Isn't Enough*, and *My Mother Worked and I Turned Out Okay*.

Expectant parents and parents of newborns also have their share of helpful humorous instruction manuals, including *Welcome to Club Mom* and *The Parent's Dictionary*. Books like these help you realize the number of times in your parenting life you ask, "Where's the bathroom?" and "Can I call you back?"

People who tell jokes for a living are called comedians. You do not have to be a comedian to use humor in parenting, but we parents can gain perspective from such performers. Listen, for example, to Bill Cosby in *Fatherhood*.

My eight-year-old was given to me just for love because she certainly doesn't do anything. The new American father has more responsibilities than ever, but children seem to have fewer. Ask any eight-year-old why she can never bring herself to do her chores and she will reply, "But I caaan't. I'm only a little person." This little person who can jump rope nonstop for twenty-seven minutes says that her chores are too great a strain on her fragile body. This little person who could ride a bicycle up Mount Washington cannot muster the strength to pick up the coat and sweater she dropped on her way to the kitchen." (p. 59)

While few of us could find the words to describe this parenting dilemma so well, most of us recognize it and can see the humor in it when Cosby tells it. As soon as a neighbor knocks on the door to play, Andrew can spring from his death bed and be fully healed of mysterious diseases that only recently interfered with his cleaning his room. Similarly, he can be "too tired" at chore time and "too awake" at bedtime, even when they occur in the same hour. Such situations have infuriated me, but I do see the humor in them, thanks to Mr. Cosby.

*After I watch or read something amusing about parenting,
I try to recall experiences I have known that are similar.
This helps me use the information from the media
as a catalyst to enhance my vision of the funny things in my life.*

There are several movies that address the issue of parenting—or the lack thereof—from *Kramer vs. Kramer* to *Honey, I Shrunk the Kids*. Film companion guides, sold in bookstores, list movies by title and synopsize them to simplify your video-rental selection.

COMIC RELIEF FROM A SERIOUS WORLD

As we begin looking for funny things, they begin to surround us. A recent visit to a grocery store proved this to me. I generally don't do the grocery shopping for the family. As a man, I learned that if I don't want to do something, I just have to act pretty much like Bill Cosby's eight-year-old and pretend I can't. I have effectively failed on several grocery shopping trips so that now I am only trusted to "pick up a few items." On a particular search for those few items, my comic vision kicked into gear.

I noticed a man in the store with a cellular phone to his ear. This isn't particularly unusual. As a psychologist, I occasionally continue a call from my car into a business establishment. The man, however, was placing a call. The seeming illogic of the scene prompted me to explore the situation further. As I approached him from a safe distance, I heard him say, "Okay, dear, I'm in the frozen foods." I tried to stay far enough from him so my laughter would not interfere with his call. I was totally entertained as I followed him through the store and virtually forgot why I was there. Many others passed this fellow and failed to even notice the free entertainment provided between aisle 7 and aisle 12.

At some point during my stalking of this stranger, another comic awareness struck me. "What if Nora saw this?" My excuse as a shopping-incompetent would no longer be effective. To me, this was a clear case of technology gone amuck. I allowed myself to drift further into the comic void. I had an image of myself, in the store, cell phone in hand, consulting my wife. I saw myself being followed by a group of strangers, while using one hand to hold the phone and the other to thump watermelons, I was saying, "Is this the one, Nora, or this one?"

As I snapped out of my trance, I was in my car in the supermarket parking lot behind a woman who had stopped her car to wait for a free-wheeling shopping cart to roll in front of her. As she waited, she apparently became impatient. The next thing I knew, she began to honk her horn at the cart. My first thought was, "Now what happens if it speeds away? Will she call the police to give it a ticket?"

Even the most mundane of activities can be experienced with intense humor if we are open to it. Shortly after Fiona was born, in the middle of a Colorado winter, my wife stopped to get gas at a local convenience store. Since Fiona was asleep, Nora and Andrew went into the store to pay. In an effort to keep Fiona safe and warm, Nora left the car running and locked the doors. Of course, to assure that Fiona was both safe and warm the keys had to be locked inside the vehicle with her. By the time the firemen came to extricate Fiona, Nora was beside herself, believing she had completely dashed all chances to be mother of the year. Fiona was fine. I am still trying to help Nora find the humor in that situation.

Our children constantly provide us with raucously funny experiences, typically when they are not intended. A friend reported that her son was fascinated with the texture of bananas, so much so that he explored how the banana felt when squished in his ears. His mother said, "Don't do that. That does not feel good." The child responded, "Mommy, have you tried it?" While laughing, the mom conceded that she had not. She decided to open herself to the opportunity, and another positive parenting experience was born.

It is unfortunate that many parents fail to see their children's behavior as comic relief from an overly serious world. Even more tragically, some parents ridicule their children for their playful behaviors. I was in the mall recently and heard an apparently sane woman yell at her four-year-old, "Stop doing that! You are acting childish!" I wondered, how exactly is a child supposed to act?

Open the Door and Let Humor In

35 ACTIVITY THIRTY-FIVE ....
Family Puppets

Materials needed: brown paper lunch bags, markers or paints, yarn or felt, scrap fabrics, construction paper, scraps

These hand puppets are a breeze to create. Stick your hand inside a lunch bag before you open it out. You'll see how the bottom of the bag serves as the place to put your fingers to move the "head." The bottom is where you paint, draw, and glue your faces.

Remember, this is supposed to be fun, not an art competition. Yarn works nicely for hair, you can simply draw on facial features. If you get into it you can decorate the rest of the bag, making clothes, adding ears and arms. The puppets can be used over and over in a variety of situations.

If you're really brave, you can use the puppets in those tense moments and have them speak for you. Hopefully, they'll be able to lighten things up. It's a great way for little ones to tell Mom and Dad secret fears, or fess up to that lamp they accidentally broke without fear of angry retribution. We have friends who put on a New Year's Eve play and act out the highlights of the past year.

36 ACTIVITY THIRTY-SIX ....
Creating Comic Awareness

1. Take your child to the supermarket or any other store.
2. Seek out a potentially comic situation.
3. When you get home, tell everybody about it.

37 ACTIVITY THIRTY-SEVEN ....
Signal Flags

Materials needed: Scrap fabric or construction paper, scissors, sewing machine or tape, wooden dowels

Nora's Uncle Johnny has been commodore of a sailing club in Michigan for many years. One night as she was pulling her hair out trying to negotiate with Andrew about getting ready for school on time, she drew an idea from her nautical experience. One day after school, she and Andrew created a batch of signal flags, similar to those used by sailors. A red and a white rectangle sewn together horizontally meant "I want to watch a kid's show." A blue and yellow triangle meant "After you are dressed." Naturally, Nora created flags for "Yes," "No," and, my personal favorite, "No way on earth."

Instead of engaging in a battle of wills, escalating to shouting, whining, and crying, they enjoy the process of waving these flags frantically at each other.

To create your own flags, decide on what messages you want to send. Then decide on patterns that will represent each message. Keep the patterns simple—one, two, or three colors and basic geometric shapes. Either sew or tape your flags together. Fold over the left edge enough to create a pocket that your dowel can slip into. Sew or tape down the edge. Place your dowel into the flag and signal away. Make sure that everyone gets an opportunity to decide what messages need to be sent. Kids and parents alike may want to create flags that signal, "I need a little space," "I need some attention," or "I need a hug."

CHAPTER THIRTEEN

SETUP: GET READY for LIFE'S UNPREDICTABLE CHANGES

"If you can't make it better,
you can laugh at it."
—ERMA BOMBECK

PEOPLE HAVE SIGNIFICANTLY DIFFERENT PALLETS when it comes to humor consumption. I was talking to a parent about using humor to gain perspective on a problem he was having with his child, when he responded angrily, "I'm not a comedian or a clown. I'm a parent." I thought to myself, that's likely to be part of the problem right there.

This book is not intended to land you a spot on *The Tonight Show* or give you the skills to tell jokes on *An Evening at the Improv.* It is, however, designed to expose you to how comedy works so that the process of making people laugh is demystified. With this knowledge you are more likely to make yourself and your children laugh when other options are less attractive. Of course, there is always the risk that you will not laugh, and neither will anyone else. Worse, rather than laugh at your technique, people may laugh at you.

Just as you would expect to fall while mastering roller blading,
so should you expect to stumble
while rehearsing your humor skills.

Despite different tastes, there are humor techniques that consistently work. Comedians use three basic mechanisms to humor us—the setup, the exaggeration, and the good news/bad news technique. In addition to being comedy devices, each of these techniques can provide you and your children with new ways of perceiving the world around you and dealing with its challenges.

Preparing for Unexpected Transitions

The most classic technique is the setup. It works because of the element of surprise that invariably follows. Comedians appeal to our expectations and then fool us. They practice the art of misdirection. Setting up a joke, they cause us to lean to the left, then they deliver a punch line that sends us careening off to the right. Listen closely to a comedian sometime and see if this isn't true.

A good example is a joke we heard earlier:

Question: How do you stop a charging rhino?
Answer: You take away his credit cards.

The setup exploits the fact that the word *charging,* when used with the word *rhino* will set up the image of a rhinoceros attacking. The "credit card" response knocks us off guard.

Is it good to be knocked off guard? I think so.
Because the more misdirection experiences we have,
the more opportunities we have to respond to them.
Life's unpredictable changes become less daunting.

Furthermore, children learn that reality and perception are quite different things. Even simple magic tricks will teach them that. For example, if I make a piece of cloth disappear "before your very eyes," the cloth does not actually vanish. I use a magic technique to create the perception that the cloth disappears and reappears at my beck and call. I create the perception with a misdirection technique that, hopefully, produces awe and wonder in the hearts and minds of an audience.

Misdirection in humor works like sleight-of-hand in magic: If we are skilled in presenting the setup, we can change the way reality is perceived.

The art of misdirection teaches us that
if we change the way we perceive any given situation,
we can instantly change our emotional response to that situation.

If I perceive, for example, that my child, by striking his sister, has committed a heinous crime and deserves to be spanked, my emotional response will be that of anger. If the exact situation occurs, but I perceive that my child has used faulty thinking that needs discipline and discussion, my emotional response will be that of loving concern. Which emotional response do you think my child would prefer? Which response do you think I would prefer when I act on the emotion? Which response do you think would produce greater learning?

By the way, I took up magic recently and find that it complements humor-in-parenting skills. Whenever I have a problem with my children, I simply make them disappear.

MOVING FROM REJECTION TO HOPE

In pursuit of my ambition to be a psychologist, I applied to every doctoral program in the world. Lower Botswana State University did not scare me. If I could read the application, I was applying. After mailing a truckload of applications, I got my first response. When I received the letter from the University of California at Los Angeles (UCLA), I was very excited. As I opened it, I could feel Ed McMahon's presence in the room. With the faint sound of a drum roll in my head, the excitement mounted as I ripped the envelope open. The letter said:

Dear Applicant:

We are sorry to inform you that you have not been accepted to the University of California, Los Angeles. Best wishes in your future career endeavors.

> Respectfully,
>
> John Michaels
> (*name changed to protect the guilty*)
> Dean of the Graduate School

As I thought about what the letter meant, I felt the despair that sometimes follows rejection. I immediately tried to recall something funny and relevant. Groucho Marx came to mind. He said, "I wouldn't want to join any club that would have me for a member."

Groucho's remark allowed me to play momentarily with the possibility that UCLA was the best school, and any school foolish enough to accept me would have to be a loser. I decided at this point that I needed to set up a situation. This setup would require that I do something unexpected that would move me away from my feeling of rejection and toward a sense of hope. I concluded that I should write UCLA an appropriate response.

Dear Graduate School:

Please accept this letter of rejection of your letter of rejection. I look forward to attending on the first day of class. Please send information regarding books.

> Sincerely,
>
> Applicant—Joseph A. Michelli

Yes, of course, I actually mailed it. So what do you think they did? They wrote me another letter.

Dear Mr. Michelli:

(Aha. They're using my name. Now we are getting somewhere.)

We are most confused by your recent correspondence. To the best of our knowledge, in the history of this institution, no one has rejected our letter of rejection. *For the sake of clarification,* there is no room for you in the incoming class, and you will not graduate.

Yours truly,

John Michaels
Dean of the Graduate School

The setup was working. I was feeling loose and hopeful. My perspective had shifted from rejection to amusement. Feeling that I had nothing to lose, I decided to write another letter.

Dear John:

Thank you so much for your correspondence. You are confused. I know exactly what my intentions are. *For the sake of clarification,* as it relates to the issue of class size, I don't take up a great deal of room. With regard to graduation, someone is likely to fail, and I will just fill in for them in line. Please send information regarding books.

Love,

Joseph

You are probably wondering whether John wrote a letter in response to mine. In fact, he called me. He said, "We think you need a psych program, but it is not going to be here at the University of California, Los Angeles."

This was all right with me because the day before I had been accepted across town at the University of Southern California, a prestigious university known for its high academic standards. Don't get me wrong. I don't harbor any ill feelings toward UCLA (short for U Can't Learn Anything) since were it not for them, I would not have attended USC (short for University of Spoiled Children).

I wound up becoming friends with "John Michaels," of UCLA once I was ensconced in studies at USC. Occasionally I would travel out of the neighborhood I was living in at the time, which was noted for its low income and high crime rate, and spend time with him in Beverly Hills, known for its high-profile, well-to-do residents. A couple of years later, we were lunching outdoors at a restaurant when John asked if I remembered my application process. When I told him that I will never forget it because of the personal interest he took in me, he told me that they had actually had a meeting among members of the Department of Psychology and the Department of Security to discuss what would happen if I actually showed up on the first day of class.

There are many situations in life
that lead us down a path of frustration.
We have a choice. We can go willingly into the frustration
or we can adjust our perspective
and take a humorous approach.

Framing an Alternate Perspective

I was using the setup to cope with my own family life long before I had a name for it. I spent a lot of my childhood rushing home to see if my mom's iron was left on—something she forever believed she did—although I assure you that it never, ever happened. Each time she insisted this might be the occasion she accidentally left it on. My mother watched TV coverage of forest fires and was convinced that they were the result of someone leaving the iron on.

Given my frustration with having to return home for no reason, I unknowingly set up a situation. I was eight years old at the time. We were living in a small town in Colorado. As we headed for a vacation in California, somewhere in the middle of Arizona my mother turned to me and said, "I wonder if the iron is on." Now this was enough to bring terror into the heart of an eight-year-old boy, but I was prepared. I reached under the seat, grabbed the iron and said, "No, Mom, here it is."

At the time, my mother was not impressed. Recently, however, she bought me an iron that shuts itself off and attached a note saying, "I bet the inventor's mother is richer." She was, of course, alluding to the fact that, instead of carrying an iron halfway across the country waiting for an opportunity to create humor, this kid was in his garage designing technology that likely brought millions to his family. Did I find her comment humorous? You be the judge.

*Many of the technological breakthroughs of our time
come from a willingness to shift perspective
from problems to solutions.*

Being playful by using the setup allows you to frame an alternative perspective. It buys you time to come up with a creative solution. It merrily nudges you out of feelings of hopelessness into a place where solutions become clearer.

CATCHING THEM BY SURPRISE

Since I don't know what situations commonly plague you in the course of your family life, I can't tell you specifically what to use with your children. However, it has been helpful for me to list the common challenges I experience as a parent, such as requesting that Andrew pick up toys that have taken up residence in the living room. I have looked at my ordinary responses, which are to tell, beg, and bribe him repeatedly to pick them up. These approaches don't work effectively, most likely because he expects them now that he's heard them so many times. Instead I try to generate as many alternative and unexpected responses to each situation as I can.

In my own warped and playful mind I contemplate options such as

1. *Establishing a "No-Toy Zone" in the living room—complete with signs.*
2. *Warning that misplaced toys will be auctioned off to family members.*
3. *Designating the living room as a "Goodwill Drop-off Zone."*

From my brainstorming session, I will choose the option that Andrew is least likely to expect. Once I choose it, I will spring the option on him in an effort to make the living room livable again.

> *The key to an effective setup*
> *is to do something completely unexpected,*
> *which breaks down a child's resistance to change.*

You can post novel signs rather than having to repeatedly "nag" your children about household responsibilities. How about these playful messages?

❖ If you drop it, pick it up.
❖ If you use the last of it, replace it.
❖ If it rings, respond to it.
❖ If it cries, love it.
❖ Your mother is not your employee.

♣ The sooner you can take care of yourself, the sooner you can be on your own.

Are you continually doing the same things even though they don't work and then blaming your children for your frustration? Do the unexpected. Let me know how it works.

I recently received an electronic mail message from a mother who wanted to share some inventive "Toddler Property Laws." Reading them takes me from frustration to amusement in a matter of seconds.

♣ If I like it, it's mine.
♣ If it's in my hand, it's mine.
♣ If I can take it from you, it's mine.
♣ If I had it a little while ago, it's mine.
♣ If it's mine, it must never appear to be yours in any way.
♣ If I'm building something, all the pieces are mine.
♣ If it looks like mine, it is mine.
♣ If I saw it first, it's mine.
♣ If you are playing with something and you put it down, it automatically becomes mine.
♣ If it's broken, it's yours.

By taking the time to do something unpredictable, we give ourselves breathing space from our initial negative or pessimistic reaction and increase the likelihood that we will come upon a more effective parenting strategy.

Finding a way to use the setup in parenting erases powerlessness through play, thereby opening up new options for problem-solving. Some folks yell at the darkness; others turn on a light. Ned Rorem said, "Humor is the ability to see three sides of one coin." When dealing with your children, sometimes two sides just aren't enough.

Open the Door and Let Humor In

38 ACTIVITY THIRTY-EIGHT ....
Ring and Run Humor Baskets

We also call this our humor care package. This activity is one of my family's favorites. We love to share our laughter and good times with our friends. To begin, take a box or basket and give it a little decoration. It can be as simple or as elaborate as you want. We like to add balloons and lots of color. In the basket assemble any of the funny stuff you've run across or made in the activities that have preceded this one. OK here are some ideas for you novice ring and runners.

- ✣ *Smiling face sugar cookies with big red frosting clown noses,*
- ✣ *Some funny pictures the family has drawn,*
- ✣ *Favorite comics cut out of this week's newspaper,*
- ✣ *Groucho Marx glasses,*
- ✣ *Joke book (handmade or store bought),*
- ✣ *Aluminum can with contents that spring out when opened,*
- ✣ *Silly hats (again, made or bought),*
- ✣ *Secret messages with directions on how to decode,*
- ✣ *IOUs to the next comedy movie that comes to the theater.*

After you have assembled your basket/box, go to your neighbor or friend's home, set your humor care package on the porch, ring the bell, and RUN.

39 ACTIVITY THIRTY-NINE ....
Humor File

In our home we have created several file drawers full of humorous material. This material has been gleaned from joke books, cartoons, junk mail, funny news headlines, funny pictures, books on humor, funny sayings, and amusing e-mail messages.

Each family member is charged with the mission of seeking and capturing material he or she thinks is funny and adding it to the collection. Fiona has not contributed yet to humor material retrieval, but since she is only one and a half years old, we figured we would give her more time.

Much of the material in our humor drawer is family humor, but all kinds of humor are accepted. Material from the humor file is used in a variety of activities, like the one listed below. Once used for another activity, the humor material often finds a final resting place back in the humor file.

40 Activity Forty ....
Family Fun Bulletin Boards

A cork bulletin board is prominently placed in our house. This board contains an ever-changing series of funny pictures drawn by family members, new cartoons, and inspirational or funny sayings. Materials rotate off the board into the humor file, and new material replaces it.

You might consider posting "funny stuff" on a bulletin board, your refrigerator, or your forehead for that matter. There is a great deal of humorous material now being posted on the World Wide Web. Some of it isn't funny, but a number of quality web addresses are listed in the resource appendix at the back of this book.

The day has come when instead of placing our children's preschool artwork on our refrigerator, we are able to publish it on the Internet for every stranger in the world to see. I cannot for the life of me decide whether that's a good thing or a bad thing.

CHAPTER FOURTEEN

EXAGGERATION: CATCH YOUR BREATH and BROADEN YOUR PERSPECTIVE

"Exaggerate a little.
A tall tale in the service of humor is a noble thing indeed."
—DAVID GARFINKEL

IT WAS A TUESDAY. I was seven years old and had decided that I wanted to take a day off school. The rule in our house was that you had to have a fever or other observable signs of disease in order to stay home. I had tried to produce other convincing symptoms without success. My last hope was to go with the fever option.

Since my mother made sure that I didn't warm the thermometer against the radiator, I thought that creating friction inside my mouth would be my best strategy. In the process, I bit the thermometer. The glass shattered and mercury dribbled from my mouth. As I was rushed to the hospital with possible mercury poisoning, I realized that exaggeration could produce powerful and unexpected results.

There was no school for me that Tuesday, but there was also no play. Sometimes there is a price to pay for success.

USING CATASTROPHE TO MAKE A POINT

Much of Bill Cosby's skill as a storyteller is his ability to exaggerate parenting to the extent that the exaggeration appears real. In our lives, we do the same thing. We frequently catastrophize difficulties as if they were the worst any human being could experience. Often we become so invested in our problems that we fail to see that they are manageable. But exaggeration can work in our favor and provide a strong benefit. In the middle of a difficult situation, exaggeration can give us a broadened perspective. An example is the age-old saying:

*"I found it wasn't so bad to walk in my shoes
when I met a man who had no feet."*

In the 1970s television situation comedy *Sanford & Son*, Fred Sanford, played by Red Foxx, was faced with a number of rather ordinary difficulties. In response them, he invariably placed his hand to his chest calling out to his deceased wife, "This is the big one, Elizabeth. I'm coming to join you."

As parents, we often respond this way to our children's misbehavior, as if we were facing the end of civilization as we know it. Clients come into my office and make such extraordinary declarations as, "If my child doesn't quit bedwetting, I'm going to die." Or "My child's tantrums are killing me."

Wanting to put the picture in perspective, I generally respond with something like, "How exactly do you see your death following from your child's behavior?"

I am frequently charged with challenging the beliefs clients hold that bring pain into their lives. Most of the time these beliefs are merely negative exaggerations:

All-or-Nothing Thinking. Believing that in order for something to be all right, it must be experienced or accomplished perfectly. *"If I don't teach my child perfect manners, I'm a worthless parent."*
Catastrophizing. Thinking about the worst possible set of outcomes. *"If I don't spend more time with my child, he is going to end up in prison as an adult."*

Overgeneralization. Concluding that similar negative experiences will occur in unrelated circumstances. *"I have been messing up a lot at work lately. I'm sure I'm messing up my kids, too."*

Shoulds and Musts. A constant perception of having to do things that are actually subject to choice. *"I should be doing a better job reading to my children. I must start a new night-time ritual."*

Emotional Reasoning. Believing that one's feelings predict reality. *"I feel scared about having another child. I know something bad is going to happen to it."*

Invalidating the Positive. Trusting only negative information and ignoring the positive. *"Thank you for the compliment about my parenting, but you should have seen how poorly I handled things at home."*

Jumping to Negative Conclusions. Drawing a negative conclusion based on limited information. *"I am not really sure what is happening here, but I don't think I am doing this right."*

Personalization. Taking things personally that are not intended as such. *"The teacher says the class needs to work on the school play. I know she means I should be spending more time working with my child on his part in the program."*

Making the Negative Embellishment Positive

These patterns of thinking reflect distortions that can produce significant emotional distress. I am convinced that if more people used exaggeration techniques positively, we would have less need for therapists. This would not be good for me professionally, but beneficial to the human psyche in general. This technique is rarely used in humorous ways, but it can be.

For example, if Sonya, an adolescent, says, "Everyone hates me," she certainly believes this is true and walks through life as if it *were* true. A therapist can help her recognize this distorted exaggeration for what it is and assist her in getting to a point where she acknowledges that "Although a few people don't seem to like me, that doesn't mean everyone hates me."

Once she accepts this change in perspective, she might even playfully exaggerate the situation herself, rephrasing the very same concept into: "Of the 600,000,000 people currently residing on the planet, more than 599,999,000 don't know me well enough to hate me. A healthy percentage of the remaining thousand probably don't hate me." Perspective is everything.

In another situation, a 14-year-old client was referred to me by a fellow doctor. The girl had been hiccuping nonstop for more than a week. Without success the doctor had tried various medications, then sent her to me. When she came to my office accompanied by her mother, I was somewhat apprehensive. I'd been treating patients for approximately 13 years and had never treated a chronic hiccuper.

When the girl came in, she said, "I (hiccup) have a problem (hiccup). I can't stop (hiccup) hiccuping."

As the girl continued to hiccup, she and her mother looked at me as if I might say or do something profound. Feeling uncomfortable, I asked myself, "What would a good doctor do if he were here now?" What would the doctors on *Chicago Hope* or *ER* do? (This is a handy technique to use when you are completely lost. And it works well for parents, too. You can ask, "What would Ward Cleaver or Claire Huxtable say at a time like this?")

I decided to use exaggeration to encourage hope on the part of the girl and her mother. I started by suggesting that I treat this all the time, as if my waiting room were filled with hiccuping patients. I clarified that the girl had been hiccuping for one week. I noted that I just talked with a patient in my office who had been hiccuping for a day and he was hiccuping better than she did. She looked at me as if she had reached the bottom of the barrel in health care.

I then asked her to exaggerate her symptoms and make them worse. She began hiccuping louder, faster, faster, louder. For a moment, I thought she was going to pass out. I then informed her that we had run out of treatment time for the day. I commented that she had made her symptoms worse and wondered if she could make them better.

Several days later, the girl's mother called. Initially I thought she was calling for a refund. Instead, she was informing me that her daughter was no longer hiccuping. I masked my shock. She asked, "Why has the hiccuping stopped?" Although the question may have been obvious, the answer certainly wasn't to me. As I thought of ways to answer the question, I decided that any good doctor would answer it in terms that he hoped his patient would not understand.

Fumbling, I said, "Well, she had a natural biofeedback experience. She gained voluntary control over what she once thought was an involuntary muscle."

This story implies that I help people cure themselves in just one session, which for the most part is exaggeration personified. Actually, only managed care companies think I can help people that quickly.

Children are experts at embellishment. Their worlds are filled with it in the form of cartoons, TV programs, and books. Make-believe and fantasy often magnify human qualities—even those of animals or inanimate objects. If you have watched Saturday morning cartoons, you understand clearly how often children are exposed to overstatement.

The Roadrunner, for example, runs faster than ACME rockets and defies gravity as he dominates Wile E. Coyote. Bugs Bunny uses far-fetched powers to befuddle Elmer Fudd. *Sesame Street* and *Barney* both embellish and overstate their situations—all to make a point. Whether it's Big Bird's size or the Power Rangers' physical skills, children who watch television are entertained on a daily basis by a suspension of reality and enhancement of the real world in which they live.

EMBELLISHING TO COPE WITH LIFE

Because of their exposure to exaggeration, children begin to use the technique not only in play but to cope with life. I remember having a long discussion with Andrew after he insisted that milk had been thrown off the table by his imaginary friend, Hermie. The discussion was rich with detail. When he realized that he was not convincing me, he laughed and said, "Well, would you believe that Hermie wanted the milk, and I was throwing it to him?"

When my wife Nora was 10 years old, she asked for an elephant for Christmas. She wanted to be a zookeeper. She believed that an elephant would not only be a good pet, but that it would provide excellent experience for her career. When her father firmly rejected the idea, she countered with a request for a pony. When the pony idea failed, she requested a puppy, which ultimately found its way under the tree. She had really only wanted a puppy, but suspected that the exaggerated requests would allow room for negotiation. That's an awfully clever ploy for a 10-year-old, don't you think?

Social psychologists have referred to this phenomenon as the "door in the face" effect, wherein you make an exaggerated request that you expect will be denied and thereby increase the likelihood that a reasonable request will later be accepted.

Here is a letter written by a female college student who clearly understood the power of exaggeration:

Dear Mom and Dad:

I would have written sooner but my stationary was burned in the fire. I am out of the hospital now. Thank God for that boy who rescued me. Did I mention I am living with him? You know you have always wanted to be grandparents, and you will be happy to know that you will be soon.

Love,
Sue

P.S. My health is perfectly fine. There was no fire. I have no boyfriend, and I am living in the same old place. I am not pregnant, but I did get a C in biology and a B in chemistry, and I just wanted to put it into perspective.

SHIFTING OUT OF ANGER

There is a Zen proverb that states that if you put an animal in a cage that is too small, it will balk and fight; but if you make the cage large enough, the animal will lie in peace. The next time you feel oppressed or devastated by a trying situation, exaggerate. Find out how expansion helps you catch your breath and how it provides both distance from the blow and time for you to make an appropriate decision.

The ability to step back from our problems is needed in parenting,
particularly when gaining perspective means
shifting out of our anger in the midst of disciplining.

I exaggerate my everyday parenting problems on purpose—to amuse myself and to reduce my frustration. When I go into Andrew's bathroom after his bath, I try to imagine that he could have splashed more water out of the tub than he actually did. I have images of the entire room, with the exception of the bathtub, filled with five feet of water. The room in my mind functions as an indoor pool with floating toys bobbing over the toilet and beyond the sink. My mental image helps me realize that things could be worse.

Open the Door and Let Humor In

41 ACTIVITY FORTY-ONE ....
Make an Official Joy List of Exaggerations.

Materials needed: Paper, pencils, pens, crayons, or paints

1. With your family, construct a list that reflects the joy of exaggeration the family has experienced while together. For nonreaders, draw or take pictures.
2. When you or someone in your family needs a lift, consult the list and, when possible, re-experience one of the activities already on it.

42 ACTIVITY FORTY-TWO ....
Keep Video Camera and Tapes Accessible

The number of videotapes sent to programs like *Funniest Home Videos* is evidence that people enjoy capturing funny aspects of home life on video. Have you ever considered having a video camera and tape available, not only to chronicle the blowing out of candles or the opening of presents but just for silly moments? Great opportunities exist to inconspicuously videotape such times. These situations might occur when families are together laughing during a board game, or you and your child are being inanely joyful in play.

Have you tried dressing up in funny outfits and turning on the video? Warning: With the protection of a disguise, the "ham" is liberated.

43 ACTIVITY FORTY-THREE ....
Develop a Humorous Trademark or Collection

Everyone needs a trademark. It helps exaggerate who we are. For Zorro it was a slashing *Z* made with his sword. For the Lone Ranger, it was "Hi Ho Silver . . . away!" For Santa it's the red suit and reindeer. For me, it is my assortment of ties. People who know me know about my strange collection of funny ties. My clients, coworkers, and family experience my humor through my neckwear. For me, ties are the perfect socially acceptable manifestation of my identity as a fun-loving person. Ties reflect truly nonfunctional formality (if you exclude catching spilled food). However, I view them as a billboard for my sense of humor. They say to the world, "I am a doctor. Take me seriously, if you dare."

I have friends with trademark fun collections, including frog figurines, Betty Boop memorabilia, and Tasmanian Devil shirts. These collections allow others to engage a playful side of themselves and give their families an opportunity to easily identify the child within each adult. I have been working with Andrew to identify his trademark. So far, it's Superman—and from my perspective, it is fitting.

CHAPTER FIFTEEN

GOOD NEWS/BAD NEWS: REDUCE STRESS and FIND SILVER LININGS

"Tragedy and comedy are but two aspects of what is real,
and whether we see the tragic or the humorous
is a matter of perspective."
—DR. ARNOLD BEISSER

A FRIEND'S FOUR-YEAR-OLD SON was excited to have captured a cricket in the front yard. When he brought it in to show his mother, his two-year-old sister snatched it from his hand and stuffed it in her mouth. All that could be seen were its two little back legs protruding from her lips. The good news for the boy was that he had, for a moment, captured a cricket; the bad news was his sister's apparent robbery of it. The good news for his sister was that she got her brother's new toy; the bad news, not all things are designed to go in your mouth. The good news for their mother was that her daughter did not swallow the cricket; the bad news was that she had partially chewed the cricket. For the cricket, well, no good news there.

AND THE GOOD NEWS IS?

Most of us are familiar with this technique. Comedians, frequently with cigar in hand, state in a Groucho Marx voice, "I got some good news, and I got some bad news." They then ask us to pick whichever news we would like to hear. Of course, they have a setup working off either choice. As you already know, as parents we don't always get to choose between bad news and good news.

A number of years ago I spoke at a national conference on humor. I had been speaking at small local gatherings for years, and was now going to speak alongside some heavy-hitters in the field. No longer did I have to pay people at Denny's to listen to me.

I was so anxious about my opportunity that I purchased an $800 Italian silk suit. I figured that if the material I was speaking wasn't any good, at least the material I was wearing would be first-rate. Buying the suit sentenced me, then a bachelor, to eat macaroni and cheese for several months.

I packed my sacred suit and departed for Chicago. At the baggage claim area, I experienced the bad news: My bag flew open upon impact with the luggage carousel, and, as it circled, my suit was shredded before my eyes. I lapsed into disaster thinking. Now that this had happened, I most likely wouldn't get ground transportation to my hotel. My room would likely not be reserved. I probably had misunderstood the invitation to be at the conference in the first place.

Determined to turn my thinking around and to find the good news in this situation, I watched my suit and bag circle the carousel. Then it came to me. The good news was that of all the times I had traveled for business, this was the only time my bag had come out first. This made me laugh and led me to think about several other amusing events. I recalled a passenger on a short commuter flight who was the only one aboard the plane. When he went to pick up his luggage, he discovered that it had been routed to another city. The good news was that I wasn't him. I also realized that, despite my traditional bachelor packing, this time I had actually packed freshly washed clothing, which was a relief since my luggage explosion had put all my underwear on display. I knew that this would be good news to my mother, because she always said, "If you are ever in an accident make sure your underwear is clean."

I decided to risk everything. I wore the ripped suit to the speaking engagement. My shredded clothing was a greater success than anything I had to say at the humor conference. Upon returning home, I showed my suit and receipt to an airline representative who gave me the good news: I would be reimbursed $800 and no macaroni and cheese would be consumed in my house for a very long time.

Getting myself to laugh at that particular incident was easier than it was when Andrew, at age two, took a serious spill. He was on my shoulders at Disney World when he reached down and knocked my glasses off my face. As I grabbed for the falling glasses, he leaned back and fell to the ground. Fortunately, within moments, a flight-for-life medical helicopter transported him to the local trauma center where he was examined and found to be perfectly fine. For a while after this episode, I berated myself and catastrophized the situation, considering myself to be a deficient parent. One day I was finally able to adjust my perspective. The bad news was that Andrew had fallen. The good news was that he was fine. Furthermore, he was the only kid that day to get a unique ride at Disney World—his personal medical helicopter—and he didn't have to wait in line.

I enjoy challenging my friends to come up with good news when disaster strikes. I know that if they can find it, they will be less stressed and better able to cope with the situation. In the long run, they are going to be healthier people.

The challenge was on when my friend's two-year-old child was playing in the yard with their dog. When she went to check on her child, she saw that the dog and child had been sharing the dog's food. She proudly told me that she was delighted to discover that the child was eating the dog's food, as opposed to other options that lay in the yard.

In another situation, a friend's seven-year-old had been quiet for a long time in her room. When her father checked on her, he observed that she had given the family dog a new hair style. The bad news was that the dog was virtually sheared. The good news? Dad had intervened before the hair-coloring kit or curling iron could be used. He and his daughter still laugh about the incident.

Good news/bad news discussions teach our children
how to admit mistakes and acknowledge problems
without becoming overwhelmed by or preoccupied with them.
They learn that the making of blunders
is an opportunity for growth and learning.

From Mistake to Betterment

Learning to make parenting lemons into lemonade is the essence of the good news/bad news technique. During "guy time" with Andrew, I sometimes use *The Blunder Book, Colossal Errors, Minor Mistakes, and Surprising Slip-Ups That Have Changed the Course of History,*[16] by M. Hirsh Goldberg. It chronicles many of the world's biggest mistakes. It also points out how many of these mistakes led to significant advancements for society. For example in 1928 at a London Hospital, a researcher by the name of Alexander Fleming was experimenting with bacteria cultures. One day before leaving the office he accidentally left some of his research near an open window. The next day when he returned, he discovered that small pieces of fungus had blown in through the window and landed on the bacteria cultures. This was apparently bad news for Mr. Fleming. But as he examined the situation more closely, he noticed that the bacteria were growing everywhere except where the fungus had landed. This led him to explore the use of fungus to stop the growth of bacteria. Later he would be dubbed "Sir" Fleming for his contribution to the development of penicillin, a drug that was being prescribed for 60 percent of all patients in the United States by 1950.

Goldberg's book also chronicles the accidental use of microwave technology for cooking as well as the error that led to the galvanization process for rubber. As in life, technical mistakes can lead to important breakthroughs.

> *FROM GOOD NEWS TO BAD NEWS TO GOOD NEWS:*
> *A baby was born, and all who knew her were happy.*
> *Later they found out that the baby was blind*
> *and were greatly saddened.*
> *When the baby, Helen Keller, made her contribution to the world,*
> *all were happy again.*

Bad news is often an opportunity to find bridges to the good. Working with cancer patients—particularly children diagnosed with incurable cancer—I have seen good come to a family from what would appear to be complete disaster. A child dies but the family goes on to start a campaign to raise money for cancer research for children. Another child dies but his organs are donated to another child who is then able to live.

TURNING LIFE'S BAD NEWS INTO GOOD

When I first started my professional career, I worked with terminally ill children at a hospice home and took my job very seriously. Every day I would shine my armor and get off my white horse to go to work. My rescuer complex didn't impress these children, however. I would sit waiting to have one of them come talk to me about the bad news in their lives—their diagnosis, the future of lost opportunities, even death.

But, I noticed that the children were too busy playing to engage me in conversation. One day I bumped into a child named Anthony, and he asked if I was all right. I thought this was a strange question for a terminally ill child to be asking me. When I said, "Yes, why?" he said, "You just look so depressed sitting here all alone."

Anthony convinced me to get out of my doctor suit to share jokes, laughter, and life. He and I became close friends in the three months we played together. His disease and ensuing death taught me that life is too short to take too seriously. Early in our relationship he noted that I was more dead than he would ever be. He was right. I had been experiencing each day as if I wanted to avoid dying rather than engaging myself in living.

It was because of my perspective shift regarding Anthony's "bad news" that I came to develop the humor perspective that I continue to share with my family, friends, and clients. Although my son, Andrew, is still very young, we frequently discuss things that initially appear to be bad news and together look for the bridges we can build to reach the good—the proverbial silver lining we can find in the midst of the dark cloud.

My young son and I talk about mistakes we've made.
We confess them to one another,
and the camaraderie that results is overwhelming.

Recently, Andrew reported the bad news was that he had become frustrated with his sister and hit her. When asked what good came from the mistake of punching her he replied, "I learned that she's old enough to punch back."

Open the Door and Let Humor In

44 ACTIVITY FORTY-FOUR ....
Good News/Bad News

At a family gathering, take turns filling in the blanks. See how many different situations come up and what laughter is produced in remembering these situations.

The bad news is _____ .

The good news is _____ .

My blunder was _____ .

It makes me laugh to think of_____ .

The good that can come from this is _____ .

45 ACTIVITY FORTY-FIVE ....
Celebrate Unusual Holidays

In an effort to be somewhat avant garde, we have added many holidays to those we used to celebrate. There is a proliferation of commemorative days, and we have begun to celebrate our favorites. These holidays, which are listed in *Chase's Annual Events*,[17] include:

January: *National Oatmeal Month*
Sherlock Holmes' Birthday
National Nothing Day

February: *National Grapefruit Month*
Bean Throwing Festival (Setsubun, Japan)
French Fry Day

March: *National Pig Day*
          Bang Clang Day
          National Goof-Off Day

Our family's celebration of the Bean Throwing Festival has certainly been more popular than our celebration of the World Cow Chip Throwing Championship, which occurs in late April. I'm not sure why—perhaps because we have thrown some cow chips before their prime.

You can create your own playful holiday—perhaps a Good News/Bad News Day, during which you do nothing but exchange good news/bad news situations.

A friend of ours annually celebrates the winter night when she and her family had a power outage. The family had such an enjoyable night in their home huddled in blankets and telling stories by candlelight that they replicate the event, as best they can, each year.

46 ACTIVITY FORTY-SIX ....
Cartoon or Humor of the Day

You may wish to either begin or end your day with a cartoon or humorous quotation. We post our quotes on a chalkboard near our humor board. Since we don't have a "fresh catch of the day" or "blue plate special" at our house, this seemed like a good use of the chalkboard.

A similar purpose is served by daily calendars with inspirational or upbeat messages imprinted on them and books of humorous sayings, such as Allen Klein's, *Quotations to Cheer You Up When the World is Getting You Down,* or Patty Wooten's *Heart, Humor and Healing.* We also include perspective-building snippets on our chalkboard such as those found in Helen Bland's *Life is Too Short.* The author writes that life is too short to fight over the remote control, the toothpaste tube, who left the lights on, who left the cage open, or who gets a particular parking space.

CHAPTER SIXTEEN

USING HUMOR RESPONSIBLY

"To every thing there is a season . . .
a time to weep, and a time to laugh."
—ECCLESIASTES 3: 1 AND 4

I WAS PRESENT when Sheila brought her new boyfriend, Mike, to a party with her colleagues. Other than Sheila, Mike knew no one at the gathering. Partly from anxiety and partly owing to a lack of sensitivity, Mike told jokes all night. By the time the evening was over, he had mowed down every gender, race, culture, and religion with his attempts at humor. Most significantly, he alienated Sheila, with whom he was never seen again.

From preschool through college, children are constantly learning to manage their relationships with others. As adults we continue to refine our skills in both intimate and nonintimate relationships throughout our lifetimes. Humor skills are advanced and sophisticated aspects of human communication, and learning to use them constructively sometimes requires a little work.

Uncovering the Intent of Our Humor

Given the embarrassing situations we sometimes suffer through with our kids, it is no wonder that parents try to curb the humor of children. However, our efforts to do so are often misguided.

Our tendency is to fail to acknowledge
our child's magnificent powers of observation
and ability to perceive the absurdities and incongruities of life.
We simply tell him that his behavior is wrong, inappropriate,
or better neither seen nor heard.

It isn't easy to reinforce that humor and laughter are wonderful and essential while at the same time teaching skills concerning the timing and situational factors involved in sharing humor. But think for a moment about how you felt when your parents acknowledged your magnificent powers of observation instead of reprimanding you for some of the things you said and did.

Many parents are concerned about the frequency with which exaggeration is used, particularly by younger children. They fear that use of humor may condone lying or conscious distortion and that their children will not be able to distinguish between socially appropriate (adaptive) and inappropriate (manipulative) uses of humor.

Used negatively, humor can deride, criticize, or injure a person, and few children escape this unfortunate brand of so-called amusement. Positive humor is the type we get from humorists like cartoonist Charles Schultz, the creator of "Peanuts," who said, "If I were given the opportunity to present a gift to the next generation, it would be the ability of each individual to laugh at himself." Positive humor has the power to reduce conflict, provide you time to examine consequences for your children's inappropriate behavior, and create a home environment of warmth and joy. But humor skills are only as good as the intent of the person using them.

Teaching our children the essence of intent
is integral to who they become in this life.

DEFINING CONSTRUCTIVE AND DESTRUCTIVE HUMOR

For humor to be positively used, distinctions between constructive and destructive humor must be grasped. I developed my own list of differences, which hangs in a prominent place in our home. I use it to remind myself of the distinctions and review it with Andrew, to help him remember, too. Perhaps you will also want to post a list.

Constructive Humor:

* *provides support*
* *enhances the esteem of those involved in it*
* *is inclusive of others*
* *explores truth and vulnerability*
* *challenges stereotypes*
* *relaxes people*
* *encourages creative thinking*
* *produces a safe and enthusiastic environment*
* *builds bridges*

Destructive Humor:

* *provides anxiety*
* *excludes others*
* *breaks down communication*
* *encourages rigid thinking*
* *creates a frightening environment*
* *injures people emotionally*
* *reduces self-esteem*

Knowledge of the context in which humor takes place is instrumental in using it constructively. The areas to be addressed to encourage constructive content and happy consequences are relationship, rapport, setting, and timing.

Your Relationship with Another Person. Humor is a form of conversation. As is the case with all social communication, it is dependent upon the nature of your relationship with the other person. Just as you might teach your children to treat strangers differently than close family, so should you teach differences in the way humor should be communicated.

I noticed two adolescent boys playing basketball together on a court near me. During their game they made fun of one another's ability and taunted one another playfully. When two other boys challenged them and started saying the same kinds of things they had said to one another, the shoving began.

Relationship Relies on Rapport. Our children need to be taught that not everyone enjoys being with people who joke with them. Learning to not joke with people who don't like it is a lesson in rapport.

In my clinical practice, I may carry a book such as *Everything Men Know About Women* into therapy. If the client asks about the book or shows interest in the title, I may leaf through it, showing that it consists of blank pages. If the client doesn't ask or seem amused, I may conclude that humor— at least, this kind of humor—will not work with this person at this time.

> *It is important that we teach children*
> *to look at and listen to how others respond to humor—*
> *the same way we teach them to cross the street.*

If a car is coming, let it pass; then cross the street when the light turns green. Watch how comfortable others feel about humor. If a joke is not well received, let it pass. Take small steps to bring another joke into your relationships with friends. Wait until the light turns green.

A neighbor friend of Andrew's never seemed to laugh at Andrew's attempts at humor. It seemed the less he responded, the more Andrew tried to get him to laugh. Andrew ultimately gave up the battle and decided that he and the other child had less in common than he had hoped. They seem to respect each other but don't make special efforts to play together.

Ensuring the Appropriate Setting and Time. In addition to knowing with whom to share humor, it is equally important to determine the appropriate place to use it. There are settings where joking or kidding around with friends may be acceptable—say, the playground. And there are other settings in which it is not—say, during a class exam. It may be fine at a party of peers, but not suitable at a party at your father's boss's house. In appropriate settings, humor does not detract from the purpose of the activity or the experience of others.

I remember getting kicked out of class along with my friend Ron for joking in sixth grade. To make matters worse, when we were serving our time in the coat room, Ron began acting silly with the other children's coats. Apparently, our laughter was disruptive to the classroom and the remainder of our sentence had to be served in the principal's office. Some lessons take longer to learn than others.

Some children believe it is inappropriate to laugh or share humor. Perhaps they, too, got caught laughing in the wrong place at the wrong time. The effects of this view are particularly noticeable in people who cover their mouths when they laugh. Somewhere they got the message that hearty laughing was a social disgrace.

For the most part, I laugh very politely and attempt not to draw any attention to myself. When I'm alone and something strikes me funny, like looking in the mirror, I let my laugh roll. This exaggeration tends to make me laugh more. Fiona has a forceful, drawn-out, belly laugh. I'm working on being able to laugh like her.

The teacher in us comes out most often when our children are doing something "wrong" or "inappropriate." We forget to be teachers of humor and to make a conscious effort to encourage their laughter. We also forget that sometimes they are our teachers.

> *Just as we need to teach our kids the boundaries*
> *of certain behavior, we also need to show them*
> *where play and humor are boundless.*

GUIDELINES FOR HUMOR IN RELATIONSHIPS

Reviewing with your kids the appropriate use of humor in relationships can help them learn how to form, strengthen, and manage interactions with others. There are three guiding rules for me: Begin by drawing a joke toward yourself. If you decide to joke about someone, make sure it's someone you know well who is likely to laugh at it, too. Finally, the focus of your joke should not be anything the other person cannot change in five minutes.

Draw a joke toward yourself. During the Abraham Lincoln-Stephen Douglas debates in the mid-1800s, Douglas publicly charged that Lincoln was "two-faced." He didn't realize that he had set up a perfect joke for Mr. Lincoln, who responded, "Ladies and gentleman of the audience, I leave it to you. If I had two faces, would I be wearing this one?"

If you're going to joke about someone, make it someone you know well who, if he hears about it, laughs too. At a large conference, Dr. Steve Dixon delivered a presentation before mine. After he made some humorous opening remarks, he announced that my presentation would follow his. Then he said, "According to the program for the conference, a cash bar will be provided during Dr. Michelli's presentation. I am not sure if this is an added bonus or a necessity."

Since he is a partner in my psychology group practice, he felt comfortable cracking that joke, which reflected a willingness to acknowledge my presentation and his uncanny ability to see a naturally occurring difference between his presentation and mine.

The focus of your joke shouldn't be anything the other person can't change in five minutes. Friends who know me well have made light of my new goatee. One asked if I was "trying to look scholarly for publicity photos." Another inquired about my razor, asking if "it had a hole in it." Yet another friend wanted to know if I had "installed a putting green on my face."

If these comments had been made by people who did not know me well, I might have taken offense. My friends' comments, however, poke fun at me in ways that show not only that they know me, but that they notice me. By targeting my goatee, they light upon something they know is not sacred to me. With a good razor, no upcoming publicity photos or need to use my face to honor my favorite pastime, I could wipe out the goatee in five minutes, tops. Now if they were to target my nose, that would be a different story. It would take a good plastic surgeon a long time to bring that down to size.

Height, weight, age, skin color, ethnic and gender-based jokes are all examples of off-limits humor.

Making fun of what is either unchangeable or changeable only through great difficulty is inappropriate for any person— friend or foe.

Open the Door and Let Humor In

47 ACTIVITY FORTY-SEVEN ....
The Good Humor Test

Create with your children several situations that they believe are funny. Give each situation the good humor test:

1. Am I the brunt of this joke, or am I making someone else the brunt?
2. If so-and-so heard this joke about her, would she laugh, too?
3. Is what I'm joking about something my friend can change in five minutes or less?
4. Would I laugh if someone I know told this joke about me?
5. How would I feel if this joke was about me?

48 ACTIVITY FORTY-EIGHT ....
Humor and Merriment Committee

Many families have adopted the weekly "family meeting" to discuss feelings, problems, and scheduling needs for family members. I know families who have reserved one family meeting per month to convene the Humor and Merriment Committee. This committee's purpose is to regularly measure the "morale" of family members and determine ways to enhance the enjoyment level of each person in the family.

The family works together to make improvements designed to increase the playfulness of the household. Suggestions that have emerged from one family's committee have included such activities as weekly trivia quizzes, developing a funny family slogan, putting on a family talent show, and playing more charades.

Family fun meetings are a formal commitment to a joyful household. Responsibility for family enjoyment goes to all members. The planning process serves as a direct family team-building activity and ensures that each individual's desires for family play are considered.

49 ACTIVITY FORTY-NINE .... Finger Puppets

Materials needed: Nontoxic markers, old glove, pom-poms, scrap material

The easy version of this activity involves simply drawing little faces on your fingers. Wiggle them around in front of the baby's face and enjoy the sound of her laughter.

The more sophisticated version involves taking an old glove or sock and creating a face or faces with pom-poms, scrap material, and markers. You can do an incredible version of "This little piggy went to market" with your new glove. Another variation on this theme is to make crazy faces on socks that are a bit too big for your child, add a little bell or some other noisemaker, place them on your children's feet, and enjoy the fun.

These puppets may also be used to practice the responsible use of humor. Use one puppet for humor that's suitable for family, another for humor that's appropriate to use with close friends, and another for humor that's appropriate for new acquaintances.

CHAPTER SEVENTEEN

The SOCIAL BENEFITS of HUMOR

"Humor is the great thing, the saving thing.
After all, the minute it crops up, all our hardnesses yield,
all our irritations and resentments flit away,
and a sunny spirit takes their place."
—MARK TWAIN

EVER SINCE NANETTE ANDERSON laughed at my joke near the swing set on the playground in kindergarten, I was hooked on humor. When it kept me from getting my face punched by the school bully in fifth grade, I praised God for its power. Art Buchwald, a popular American humorist who had a difficult childhood and who spent time in an orphanage, revealed, "I learned quickly that when I made others laugh, they liked me."

FITTING IN AND SAVING FACE

When trying to "fit in" with a new group, children often face the suspicion of group members. A child can gain at least temporary acceptance through laughter, the group's shared expression of pleasure. If a child can laugh at the humor of the group, he is identified as like-minded and begins to be perceived as affiliated with the group. Just as a public speaker might open a speech with an amusing story, our children can initiate new relationships with entertaining stories of their own—particularly if these stories are well told and brief.

Every social group, whether it's Boy Scouts or 4-H, welcomes a child who has the ability to communicate humor—a jester who can playfully express the views of the group to those perceived to be outsiders. At times, a "class clown" absorbs some of the punishment of outsiders on behalf of the group. Using humor from time to time within a social setting increases a sense of solidarity between group members. The development of a private humor collection reflects a group's identity and cohesion. Best friends and families can laugh at "inside jokes" based on their shared humor experiences, using their own humorous signs, gestures, and language.

I was watching two five-year-old boys who appeared to be meeting for the first time on a playground. One boy attempted to start up a relationship with the other by acting "silly" through exaggerated monkey sounds and gestures while swinging from the monkey bars. The other child seemed to enjoy this playful behavior, and he returned it in kind. The second boy then got the idea that they could continue their monkey antics on the swing set. He said, "Let's go be monkeys on the swing!"

The first boy said that monkeys don't swing on swings. The second boy then said, laughing, "I knew that! I was just joking!" This explanation was accepted by the first boy and later I observed them both swinging from the swing set like monkeys.

When we are relating to others, humor allows us to test the acceptability of our opinions. The ability of using humor as a means to withdraw an opinion is a rather sophisticated social skill that eliminates the need for conflict over relatively unimportant differences between people.

Humor is a social lubricant. It reduces friction and tension in daily conversation and defuses conflict.

The ability to use humor to save face is important in social interaction. The second boy could have held his ground given that it is reasonable to think that monkeys would swing on swings. This rigidity, however, would likely have dissolved any further chance of interacting with his new friend.

Some parents may feel it is dishonest to use humor to smooth interpersonal conflicts. If another child suggests that it is unreasonable to swing on a swing like a monkey, a child should respond, "Of course, it isn't. Monkeys swing from vines and cords in the jungle all the time." These parents would probably advocate being totally honest when friends ask if we like their hair, or ask how they look. They would also feel uncomfortable using a comedic technique like exaggeration with their children because it encourages conscious distortion of reality.

THE DIFFERENCE BETWEEN TACT AND LYING

Teaching children the difference between tact and lying can be difficult. Typically this distinction hinges on the importance of the issue for which total honesty is being demanded. It is also dependent upon the purpose of the interaction and who will benefit from the lack of complete frankness. If the person using the deception benefits at the other person's expense, the distortion is likely a lie. If the benefits are truly for the person hearing the distortion, or for both people mutually, distortion may be considered a refined social skill.

In the example of the two boys, the second boy was able to achieve his purpose in the interaction—to engage playfully. And no one was hurt by his response.

Tact involves responding to a question posed to you without hurting the feelings of the person who posed it. It requires the absence of brutal honesty without the presence of total dishonesty in truth, a fine line. In contrast, lying involves distorting the truth to benefit the person doing the distorting.

Tact is our verbal demonstration of social conscience.
Lying reflects a disregard for our personal conscience.

This distinction, while subtle, is particularly important as social skills often require the ability to soften feedback given in response to others without losing credibility. A classic example of the difficulty of honesty without tact is demonstrated in a movie called *Liar, Liar.* The main character, for a period of time, loses his ability to lie—even to be tactful.

Exaggeration is one form of untruthfulness. If I say an elephant is as "big as a house" or "I ate a ton of chicken," I am not being truthful. In certain situations exaggeration is useful to get perspective. At the same time, it is important that exaggeration not be used to diffuse responsibility for a problem. Children can exaggerate a problem to give themselves time to look for a solution, but in the end, they are responsible for the solution.

CHARACTERISTICS THAT DEVELOP WITH HUMOR

A child who can demonstrate humor says to others that he or she:

* *Is adaptable—flexible,*
* *Can cope with adversity,*
* *Accepts his or her own limitations,*
* *Can decrease anxieties, and*
* *Has the ability to gain perspective in difficult situations.*

A well-developed sense of humor helps a person do all those things. And don't you imagine that most of us would gravitate toward that type of person because she will help us feel better about ourselves, no matter the situation?

I have such a friend with whom I sometimes go fishing. On one fishing trip with him I'd forgotten an important item. Rather than becoming irate over my forgetfulness, he said, "That's okay. I'm getting to the point with my memory that I can hide my own Easter eggs."

Perspective-building skills like these are highly sought. If you had your choice of spending a week-long camping trip with a person who playfully responds to life's adversities or with a chronic complainer, which would you choose?

GENERIC CRISIS LINES

To gain perspective in times of crisis, there are key phrases I have adopted to help myself and others. Most of these are specific to my most common problems:

* ❖ *"You have just experienced one of my unpredictable wonders."*
* ❖ *"That is just one of the glitches left in me by the great programmer in the sky."*
* ❖ *"If it ain't fixed, I broke it."*
* ❖ *"Even though the word* manual *has the word* man *in it, I am exempt."*

Andrew and I often apply exaggeration to crisis management. When something bad happens, we do an exercise called "It Could Have Been Worse." The other day, I was fixing a lamp when the screwdriver slipped and broke the bulb. Andrew said the setup line: "Well, Dad, it could have been worse." He then followed it with: "It could have been plugged in."

Knowing me, it was a miracle that it wasn't. Best of all, instead of cursing my clumsiness, I laughed. Andrew's insight demonstrated to me that he knows some of the dangers of electricity. It also showed me that he has tools to use in the face of adversity.

Two essential points I like to remember about the social benefits of humor are:

* ❖ **Humor can be an escape mechanism or a real way to solve problems. The choice is up to you.** If we deflect everything that happens to us with humor without following it up with thought and action, we are likely using humor as an escape mechanism, in which case we will fail to solve our problems. As such, humor is no more effective than alcohol, drugs, or gambling. While it can be used for perspective-

building, humor cannot replace the need to deal with a problem directly.

❖ *One must use self-directed humor in moderation.* Constantly turning negative comments onto oneself can lose its effectiveness. Ongoing self-critical remarks only serve to undermine self-esteem and alienate the individual from the group.

When Erma Bombeck was asked about the social benefits of laughter and humor, the high-profile, well-paid author and humorist responded, "Not the least of them is a Mercedes in my garage and three children with straight teeth."

Open the Door and Let Humor In

50 ACTIVITY FIFTY ....
It Could Have Been Worse!

Apply exaggeration to crisis management. During time spent with your child, or with the entire family, play "It Could Have Been Worse." Choose a situation that happened, use the setup line, "It could have been worse." Then, follow up with an invented punch line.

This game can even be played during heinous chore time—while doing dishes, cleaning up a room, painting, setting up a campsite, driving on a car trip. If you have a portable tape recorder, you may want to record these exaggerations and play them back at a later time.

51 ACTIVITY FIFTY-ONE ....
I'm Weaker Than You Are!

During a family night, provide paper and pencil and suggest that all family members list their perception of their weaknesses. Then each member can suggest humorous ways to deal with these weaknesses when they are feeling self-conscious. If a family member is okay with it, invite other family members to come up with alternative ways to deal with their weaknesses.

52 ACTIVITY FIFTY-TWO ....
Weekend Theme Days

Friends of mine have "theme days" on weekends, often related to subjects the children are learning in school. If the kids are studying space, they may make astronaut costumes out of household items like bowls, pots, pans, coat hangers, and aluminum foil. They also prepare meals consistent with the theme, such as homemade pizzas in the shape of the planets of the solar system. How would you like to stop by that house unannounced and be greeted by a 36-year-old man wrapped in aluminum foil eating a pizza shaped like Saturn?

CHAPTER EIGHTEEN

A NEW FORM of DISCIPLINE

"I realize that humor isn't for everyone.
It's only for people who want to have fun, enjoy life, and feel alive."
—ANNE WILSON SCHAEF

IT WAS THE DAY I DECIDED TO WRITE THIS BOOK. Andrew was, as he puts it, "having a very bad day." Everything I asked him to do was met with a parent's favorite response—"No!" Time-outs were getting us nowhere. He was out of control, and I was quickly joining him. As my blood pressure rose, my temper shortened and my voice became more intense. I asked myself, "Where did this child come from and can I take him back without a receipt?"

It's been said that change comes from either inspiration or desperation. My despair forced me to disengage from the morning-long warfare. I went into his room waving a white flag, requesting peace.

Andrew began laughing and asked if I would read him a book. As he sat on my lap, I noticed that he was feverish. As it turned out, he had been feeling ill the entire morning. The same child who appeared to be my enemy just moments before was now lying quietly and contentedly in my arms.

I knew then that discipline could only be effective
in a relationship of mutual respect.
As I had been losing my regard for Andrew,
humor and play reconnected us.

With this connection, I could understand Andrew's needs better and help him gain control of himself.

GOALS AND PREPOSTEROUS SOLUTIONS

I am so much better at helping other people raise their children than I am at raising my own. Sometimes I am too close to the problems my children are having to be able to see them in their proper perspective. I can spend an entire day at the office explaining to parents that their children's behavior is perfectly normal. When I come home and see the same behavior in my children, I become concerned. Because my children matter to me, everything they do affects me. When they succeed, I feel deep pride; when they suffer, I experience sharp pain. When they misbehave, I fume.

We all know that when we discipline our children we should be calm and detached. Effective discipline requires letting go of anger and showing children the consequences that result from questionable choices. Given the emotional investment we have in our children, letting the anger go isn't always easy. In fact, it's difficult to let go of something unless you have something else to put in its place.

I have tried releasing my anger by counting to ten or leaving the room. These strategies work some of the time, but frequently my children will escalate their positions even as they follow me. I may be calming myself, but I'm doing nothing to redirect them. Finding humor during angry moments addresses the short-term needs of both parents and children.

Few things are as difficult to manage as a completely irrational child in public. A client of mine has taken a playful approach to dealing with her six-year-old's ranting behavior. She has constructed signs. One of them reads, "Please excuse his tantrum." Another: "Danger—Mood Under Repair." When her son was out of control, rather than experiencing her anger and embarrassment, she set a sign next to the child so others could read it. This prompted laughter from passersby, which did not please her child, whose angry displays stopped quickly.

When angered we frequently focus on the wrongfulness of our children's behavior without trying to understand its purpose. In the space of time between a child's misbehavior and our determination of logical consequences, a humor perspective can serve a very loving function.

*If you accept that most children misbehave to achieve a goal,
it becomes important not to simply respond to the misdeed, but
to help your children reach their goals in a more appropriate way.*

Andrew's most unreasonable and unacceptable behavior comes when he is hungry, tired, ill, or overstimulated. By taking the time to ask our favorite humor questions, Nora and I can frequently see the context in which Andrew's misbehavior is occurring.

These questions include:

❖ *Has anyone fed this child?*
❖ *Do we know anyone who would take this child away?*
❖ *Would hypnotherapy work to help this child take a nap?*
❖ *Would it be acceptable to take him to a white room with padded walls?*
❖ *If not, is such a room available for his parents?*

By asking these questions, we shift attention away from our powerlessness and focus on absurd solutions. Sometimes absurdity is a viable option to reality. When we are thinking more about solutions—even preposterous ones—we can help the child understand why he is acting out and what choices will help him get back in control.

DIVERSIONS AND DISTRACTIONS

Being a man, my only experience with birth was my own and, as an observer, the births of my children. From my observations and the impassioned reports of my wife, I surmise giving birth must be painful.

Despite the excruciating features of it, many women believe that Lamaze will help them. Don't get me wrong. I don't think that Lamaze hurts the delivery process in any way, but I am skeptical about how much pain relief it can offer during the main event. It seems like trying to drop an elephant with a fly-swatter. To my view, the benefit of Lamaze is that it gives a woman something to do as nature and gravity take over. By occupying a woman with activity, Lamaze reduces the anxiety that often interferes with the process. Well, dear reader, humor and Lamaze have a lot in common.

> *When we experience the pain of parenting,*
> *a humorous perspective can occupy us*
> *and reduce emotional reactions*
> *that get in the way of our effectiveness.*

Creating humor may not always lead to effective results while disciplining our children, but at least we are doing something from which no harm will likely come.

Fiona is at an age when she loves to pick up important things, like my wallet. If I try to get it back from her, she cries loudly. If, however, I can convince her that something else I have is of greater value (like a ball), I can make a trade without tears—most often, hers. These simple misdirections and distractions are common with babies. As children age, distractions still work, but they require more creativity.

With Andrew, we are getting to the point where "Look over there!" does not keep him from seeing the Toys R Us, Discovery Zone, or McDonald's PlayPlace across the street. In fact, he has learned so much that he now amuses Nora by saying, "Mom! Look over there! It's a diversion!"

When children get stuck in a negative loop of behavior or thinking, humor can serve to distract them out of it. When Andrew gets cranky, I'll frequently say, "Hey, Buddy, do you want to hear a joke?" I try to keep a fresh supply of riddles and children's humor in my memory for just these times. I may make up a story for him or try to get him to tell me one.

Nora's approach is somewhat different. Andrew was acting out for the entertainment of his cousins one afternoon. Nora was becoming exasperated with him. In an angry voice she said, "You are driving me crazy. You . . . " Before she finished the next sentence, she realized that her words would be both unkind and embarrassing to him. She shifted her sentence on the spot by using exaggeration. She said, "You . . . are turning my hair gray. Soon it will all be gray; then it will fall out. You will have a bald mother." Andrew found his mother's remark unexpected and began to laugh. He stopped his bald-producing behavior, and now his mother's potential baldness has become an inside joke for the two of them.

Nora can often stop his misbehavior by just pointing to her hair. She keeps the joke running. The other day she rented a video on cutting children's hair. When Andrew asked about it, without hesitation she told him she was going to use it to learn how to get his hair to fall out.

There are situations in parenting where nothing can be accomplished. The child is locked into a totally defiant posture. At these times some parents resort to physical force to break their child's wild spirit.

Humor provides the option of side-stepping a conflict
so you can address it productively on another day, at another time.
Once a child is out of that foul mood, discussion of behavior
and its associated consequences prove more effective.

Humor is not intended to make discipline more lenient— just more successful. Finding perspective, resolving anger, and defraying battles all serve the interest of raising well-mannered children.

THE GIFT OF YOUR CHILDREN'S VISION

On the occasional days that I take Andrew to school, I try to get him there before the other children, simply because he likes to be the first one there. Unfortunately, other parents don't coordinate their schedules with mine. When someone beats us to school, I am accused of being a "bad dad."

The other day was different. In the quiet moments before school with no one around but Andrew and me, he delighted me. First, we determined that I am a "head" doctor and that he wants to be a "heart" doctor. Our arrangement will be that he will send all his heart patients to me and I will send all my head patients to him.

Then, he started talking about the bathroom at school and how it had proven to him that he had superpowers. Since I had never known of superpowers being proven by a bathroom, I asked for more information.

Andrew told me that after he used the paper towels, he looked at the paper towel holder and one more paper towel rolled down. This proved to him that his vision had the power to make things move. If Andrew had been a little older I might be considering medication for him. However, the unseen force of gravity was superpower to Andrew, and his view of the world was a gift to me. Later that day, I caught myself watching the paper towel holder in my office.

Not a day goes by that I fail to notice the blessings of my children. Undoubtedly, my life would be simpler without them. There would be no need to referee battles over toys, mend scraped knees, or spend more time baiting hooks than having my line in the water. I wouldn't have to answer endless "why" questions or deal with tattling. On the other hand, I would not be able to enjoy camping in the back yard, being the fire-breathing dragon, or carrying tired bodies with angelic faces from the car to their beds.

Humor, laughter, and play are offered to us by our children as payment for the many thankless hours and duties of parenting. Tragically, many people never see the wonder of their children whose enduring enchantment, even in the worst of times, can shine as brightly as stars on a country night.

The other day Fiona, Andrew, and I were home together. Nora was on her way home. Fiona and Andrew had taken to slamming the front door. Despite my efforts to redirect them to some other activity, they persisted. Finally, I barked, "The next person to slam the door goes to their room." No sooner did I leave the room than I heard the door slam. As I came back I heard Andrew say, "Mom, you better go to your room right now."

To modify a recruiting slogan, being a parent is the toughest job you'll ever love. It is also one of the most exhausting. In addition to the joy derived from being with our children, each of us needs time away from them to be more fully able to cherish them. Finding time to nurture, pleasure, and humor yourself—alone or in the company of other adults—is central to mental health. When your cup is empty, joy is hard to find. Regular attention to your emotional needs keeps you from running critically low on essential fuels—joy, energy, and hope.

When I read books about parenting, I sometimes feel that, from the author's point of view, I could never possibly do enough to raise a healthy child. I don't agree.

The happiness and health of our children require very little.
By taking care of ourselves, finding time for them,
and nurturing joy, laughter, and humor in our homes,
we provide all the necessary ingredients.

Andrew is convinced that he will marry his sister and that they will have children with superpowers, like Batman and Spiderman. He has repeatedly told Nora and me that they will buy a house next to ours and that we will see our superhero grandchildren often. I don't have the heart to rush reality into his life just yet.

I do hope that someday Andrew and Fiona will fall in love with wonderful people, marry, and create families of their own. I hope that they will visit often and that the sounds of their laughter and the laughter of grandchildren will warm our hearts and home. If for some reason they leave and never return, Nora and I will have our family humor albums and the knowledge of our family fun to comfort us. I cannot help but believe that they will not stay gone long, because I know for a fact—families who laugh, last. Humor, play, and laughter will continue to stress-proof the lives of generations to come.

ENDNOTES

HUMOR, PLAY, & LAUGHTER

[1] Kahlil Gibran, *The Prophet,* Copyright 1923 by Kahlil Gibran, renewed 1951 by Administrators CTA of Kahlil Gibran Estate and Mary G. Gibran. Reprinted by permission of Alfred A. Knopf, Inc., pp. 17–18.

Words from *The Prophet,* by Kahlil Gibran are used by permission from The National Committee of Gibran 1951, all rights reserved.

[2] Bettie B. Youngs, *Stress and Your Child: Helping Kids Cope with the Strains and Pressures of Life,* Fawcett Columbine, New York, NY, 1995. Reprinted by permission of Ballantine Books, a Division of Random House, Inc., p. 5.

[3] Hans Selye, *The Stress of Life,* McGraw Hill, New York, NY, 1976.

[4] Wee Sing is a registered trademark of Price Stern Sloan, member of Putnam and Grosset Group, New York, NY.

[5] Arnold Glasgow, *Quotations to Cheer You Up: When the World is Getting You Down,* compiled by Allen Klein, Wings Books, New York, NY, 1991, p. 127.

[6] L. S. Berk, S. A. Tan, et al. "Neuroendocrine and Stress Hormone Changes During Mindful Laughter," *American Journal of Medical Science.* 296:390–396, 1989.

[7] William F. Fry, M.D., presentation, "The Annual Conference of the American Association of Therapeutic Humor," San Francisco, CA, 1995.

[8] George E.Valliant, M.D., *The Wisdom of the Ego,* Harvard University Press, Cambridge, MA, 1993.

[9] Foster W. Cline, M.D., *Conscienceless Acts, Societal Mayhem,* The Love and Logic Press, Inc., Golden, CO, 1995.

[10] Jerome and Dorothy Singer, *The House of Make-Believe: Children's Play and the Developing Imagination,* Harvard University Press, Boston, MA, 1990.

[11] "Gagline: The Unique Cartoon Caption Game." Invisions, Inc.

[12] Cheryl Miller Thurston and Elaine Lundberg, *If They Are Laughing, They're Not Killing Each Other: Ideas for Using Humor Effectively in the Classroom—Even if You're Not Funny Yourself,* Cottonwood Press, Fort Collins, CO, 1992.

[13] Sandra Campbell Chapin and Harry F. Chapin, "The Cat's in the Cradle." Story Songs Ltd., 83 Green Street, Huntington, NY 11743.

[14] William Bennett, ed. *The Children's Book of Virtues,* Simon & Schuster, New York, NY, 1995.

[15] John Kabat-Zinn, *Wherever I Go, There I Am,* Hyperion, New York, NY, 1994.

[16] M. Hirch Goldberg, *The Blunder Book: Colossal Errors, Minor Mistakes, and Surprising Slip-Ups that Have Changed the Course of History,* Morrow, New York, NY, 1984.

[17] Harrison V. Chase, *Chase's Annual Events,* Contemporary Books, Published Annually 1983–1993. Published annually as *Chase's Annual Events. Calendar of Events,* Chicago, IL, 1993.

HUMOR and PARENTING RESOURCES

BOOKS

Children and Parenting

Brazelton, T. Berry. *Families: Crisis and Caring*. Reading, MA: Addison-Wesley Publishing Company, 1989.

Brazelton, T. Berry. *To Listen to a Child: Understanding the Normal Problems of Growing Up*. Reading, MA: Addison-Wesley Publishing Company, 1984.

Brazelton, T. Berry. Touchpoints: *Your Child's Emotional and Behavioral Development*. Reading, MA: Addison-Wesley Publishing Company, 1992.

Brazelton, T. Berry. *Working and Caring*. Reading, MA: Addison-Wesley Publishing Company, 1985.

Cline, Foster, and Jim Fay. *Parenting with Love and Logic*. Colorado Springs, CO: Piñon Press, 1990.

Cline, Foster, and Jim Fay. *Parenting Teens with Love and Logic*. Colorado Springs, CO: Piñon Press, 1992.

Ford, Judy. *Wonderful Ways to Love a Teen . . . Even When It Seems Impossible*. Berkley, CA: Conari Press, 1996.

Hamner, Tommie J., and Pauline H. Turner. *Parenting in Contemporary Society*. Third edition. Boston, MA: Allyn & Bacon, 1995.

Joseph, Joanne M. The *Resilient Child: Preparing Today's Youth for Tomorrow's World*. New York, NY: Plenum Press, 1994.

Konner, Melvin. *Childhood*. Boston, MA: Little, Brown & Company, 1991.

Lazear, Johnathan, and Wendy Lazear. *Meditations for Parents Who Do Too Much*. New York, NY: Fireside/Simon Schuster, 1993.

Minirth, Frank, Brian Newman, and Paul Warren. *The Father Book*. Nashville, TN: Thomas Nelson, 1992.

General Humor, Laughter, and Silliness

Allen, Steve. *How to Be Funny: Discovering the Comic You*. Buffalo, NY: Prometheus Books, 1992.

Allen, Steve. *Make 'em Laugh*. Buffalo, NY: Prometheus Books, 1993.

Asimov, Isaac. *Treasury of Humor*. Boston, MA.: Houghton Mifflin Company, 1971.

Barreca, Regina. *Perfect Husbands and Other Fairy Tales: Demystifying Marriage, Men and Romance*. New York, NY: Harmony, 1993.

Barreca, Regina. *They Used to Call Me Snow White but I Drifted*. New York, NY: Viking, 1991.

Bland, Helen, et al. *Life is Too Short. . . .* New York, NY: Warner Books, 1993.

Buchwald, Art. *The Buchwald Stops Here*. New York, NY: G. P. Putnam's Sons, 1976.

Burns, George. *How to Live to Be a Hundred Years or More*. New York, NY: Putnam, 1983.

Hageseth, Christian III. *A Laughing Place: The Art and Psychology of Positive Humor in Love and Adversity*. Ft. Collins, CO: Berwick Publishing Company, 1988.

Klein, Allen. *The Healing Power of Humor*. New York, NY: Jeremy P. Tarcher, Incorporated, 1989.

Klein, Allen, compiler. *Quotations to Cheer You Up When the World is Getting You Down*. New York, NY: Wings Books, 1991.

McGhee, Paul E. *PUNchline: How to Think Like a Humorist If You're Humor Impaired*. Dubuque, IA: Jendall/Hunt Publishing Company, 1993.

Wooten, Patty, ed. *Heart, Humor and Healing*. Mount Shasta, CA: Commune-A-Key Publishing, 1994. P.O. Box 507, 96067.

Humor—Children and Parenting

Adler, Bill, compiler. *Children's Letters to Santa*. Secaucus, NJ: Carol Publishing Group, 1993.

Barry, Dave. *Babies and Other Hazards of Sex*. Emmaus, PA: Rodale Press, 1984.

Bombeck, Erma. *Family Ties*. New York, NY: Fawcett Crest Books, 1986.

Bombeck, Erma. *Motherhood, the Second Oldest Profession*. New York, NY: Bantam-Doubleday-Dell Publishing Group, 1983.

Bombeck, Erma, and Bill Keane. *Just Wait Till You Have Children of Your Own*. New York, NY: Fawcett Crest, 1971.

Cosby, Bill. *Childhood*. New York, NY: Berkley Books, 1991.

Cosby, Bill. *Fatherhood*. Garden City, NY: Doubleday & Company, 1986.

Ephron, Delia. *How to Eat Like a Child*. New York, NY: Ballantine Books, 1977.

Furman, Merrill. *The Parent's Dictionary: From Arrrrgggh! to Zzzzzzzzzz* . . . Chicago, IL: Contemporary Books, Incorporated, 1995.

Goldman, Katherine Wyse. *My Mother Worked and I Turned Out Okay*. New York, NY: Willard Books, 1993.

Hample, Stuart, and Eric Marshall, compilers. *Children's Letters to God*. New York, NY: Workman Publishing, 1991.

Hill, Deborah J. *Humor in the Classroom: A Handbook for Teachers (and Other Entertainers!)*. Springfield, IL: Charles C. Thomas, 1988.

Langer, Victor. *Surviving Your Baby and Child*. New York, NY: Macmillan Publishing Company, 1988.

Lewis, Cynthia Copeland. *Really Important Stuff My Kids Have Taught Me*. New York, NY: Workman Publishing Company, 1994.

Linkletter, Art. *A Child's Garden of Misfortune*. Greenwich, CT: Fawcett Crest, 1965.

Linkletter, Art. *Kids Say the Darndest Things*. Aurora, IL: Caroline House Publishing, 1978.

Linkletter, Art. *The New Kids Say the Darndest Things*. Ottawa, IL: Jameson Books, Incorporated, 1995.

Loomans, Diane. *The Laughing Classroom: Everyone's Guide to Teaching with Humor and Play*. Tiburon, CA: H.J. Kramer, 1993.

McPherson, John. *McPherson on Parenting*. Grand Rapids, MI: Zondervan Publishing, 1992.

Rinzler, Carol Eisen. *Your Adolescent: An Owner's Manual*. New York, NY: Atheneum, 1981.

Rogers, Fred. *Dear Mister Rogers, Does It Ever Rain in Your Neighborhood?* New York, NY: Penguin Books, 1996.

Salmans, Mary C., and Sandra Salmans. *The Working Mother's Guilt Guide: Whatever You're Doing, It Isn't Enough.* New York, NY: Penguin Books, 1992.

Sherman, James R. *The Magic of Humor in Caregiving.* Golden Valley, MN: Pathway Books, 1995.

Smith, Harold B. *Hey Dad! Are We There Yet?: One Man's Tireless Search for the Perfect Family Vacation.* Colorado Springs, CO: NavPress, 1994.

Spirson, Leslie Lehr. *Welcome to Club Mom: The Adventure Begins.* Minneapolis, MN: CompCare Publishers, 1991.

Thurston, Cheryl Miller, and Elaine M. Lundberg. *If They're Laughing, They're Not Killing Each Other: Ideas for Using Humor Effectively in the Classroom—Even If You're Not Funny Yourself.* Ft. Collins, CO: Cottonwood Press, 1992.

Play and Wordplay

Adler, Bill Jr. *Tell Me a Fairy Tale: A Parent's Guide to Telling Magical and Mythical Stories.* New York, NY: Penguin Books, 1995.

Artell, Mike. *The Wackiest Nature Riddles on Earth.* New York, NY: Sterling Publishing Company, 1993.

Bennett, Steve, and Ruth Bennett. *365 Outdoor Activities You Can Do with Your Child.* Holbrook, MA: Bob Adams, Incorporated, 1993.

Bennett, Steve, and Ruth Bennett. *Waiting Games.* New York, NY: Penguin Books, 1995.

Berg, Elizabeth. *Family Traditions.* Pleasantville, NY: Readers Digest Assoc., 1992.

Chapman Weston, Denise, and Mark S. Weston. *Playful Parenting: Turning the Dilemma of Discipline into Fun and Games.* New York, NY: A Jeremy P. Tarcher/Putnam Book, 1993.

Chapman Weston, Denise, and Mark S. Weston. *Playwise: 365 Fun-Filled Activities for Building Character, Conscience, and Emotional Intelligence in Children.* New York, NY: A Jeremy P. Tarcher/Putnam Book, 1996.

Einon, Dorothy. *Play with a Purpose: Learning Games for Children Six Weeks to Ten Years.* New York, NY: Pantheon Books, 1985.

Erickson, Donna. *More Prime Time Activities with Kids.* Illustrated by David LaRochelle. Minneapolis, MN: Augsburg Fortress, 1992.

Erickson, Donna. *Prime Time Together with Kids.* Illustrated by David LaRochelle. Minneapolis, MN: Augsburg Fortress, 1989.

Erskine, Jim, and George Moran. *Fold a Banana: And 146 Other Things to Do When You're Bored.* New York, NY: C.N. Potter, 1978.

Gerler, William R., compiler. *A Pack of Riddles.* Illustrated by Giulo Maestro. New York, NY: E. P. Dutton and Company, Incorporated, 1975.

Goldberg, M. Hirsh. *The Blunder Book: Colossal Errors, Minor Mistakes, and Surprising Slip-Ups That Have Changed the Course of History.* New York, NY: Morrow, 1984.

Hall, Rich. *Sniglets (snig 'lit): Any Word That Doesn't Appear in the Dictionary, But Should.* New York, NY: Collier Books, MacMillan Publishing Company, 1984.

Kohl, Marguerite, and Frederica Young. *Jokes for Children.* New York, NY: Farrar, Straus and Giroux, 1989.

Hoke, Helen, compiler. *More Riddles, Riddles, Riddles.* New York, NY: Franklin Watts, 1976.

Lieberman, J. Nina. *Playfulness: Its Relationship to Imagination and Creativity.* New York, NY: Academic Press, 1977.

Perry, Susan K. *Playing Smart: A Parent's Guide to Enriching, Offbeat Learning Activities for Ages 4–14.* Minneapolis, MN: Free Spirit Publishing, Incorporated, 1990.

Pipkin, Turk. *Be A Clown: The Complete Guide to Instant Clowning.* New York, NY: Workman Publishing, 1989.

Segal, Marilyn. *Your Child at Play: Birth to One Year.* New York, NY: Newmarket Press, 1985.

Silberg, Jackie. *Games to Play with Toddlers.* Mt. Rainier, MD: Gryphon House, Incorporated, 1993.

Silberg, Jackie. *More Games to Play with Toddlers.* Mt. Rainier, MD: Gryphon House, Incorporated, 1996.

Smoler, Wendy. *Playing Together: 101 Terrific Games and Activities that Children Ages 3–9 Can Do Together.* New York, NY: A Fireside Book, 1995.

Sparling, Joseph, and Isabelle Lewis. *Learning Games for the First Three Years: A Guide to Parent Child Play.* New York, NY: Walker and Company, 1979.

Stock, Gregory. *The Kid's Book of Questions.* New York, NY: Workman Publishing, 1988.

Stupid Jokes for Kids. Selected from the *Big Fat Giant Joke Book.* New York, NY: Ballantine Books, 1989.

Wilde, Larry. *The Official Smart Kids/ Dumb Parents Joke Book.* New York, NY: Pinnacle, 1977.

Wilkinson, Paul F., ed. *In Celebration of Play: An Integrated Approach to Play and Child Development.* New York, NY: St. Martin's Press, 1980.

Fun Children's Books

Base, Graeme. *Animalia.* New York, NY: Harry N. Abrams, Incorporated, Publishers, 1986.

Bennett, William J., ed. The Children's Book of Virtues. Illustrated by Michael Hague. New York, NY: Simon and Schuster, 1995.

Carle, Eric. The Grouchy Ladybug. New York, NY: HarperCollins Publishers, 1996.

Carle, Eric. The Very Busy Spider. New York, NY: Philomel Books, 1984.

Cole, Joanne. It's Too Noisy. Illustrated by Kate Duke. New York, NY: Thomas Y. Crowell, 1989.

Emberley, Ed. *Go Away, Big Green Monster!* New York, NY: Little, Brown and Company, 1992.

Geisel, Theodor Seuss. *A Hatful of Seuss: Five Favorite Dr. Seuss Stories, by Dr. Seuss* [pseud.]. New York, NY: Random House, 1996.

Geisel, Theodor Seuss. *Daisy-Head Mayzie, by Dr. Seuss* [pseud.]. New York, NY: Random House, 1994.

Geisel, Theodor Seuss. *Green Eggs and Ham, by Dr. Seuss* [pseud.]. New York, NY: Beginner Books, 1960.

Geisel, Theodor Seuss. *How the Grinch Stole Christmas! by Dr. Seuss* [pseud.]. New York, NY: Random House, 1957.

Guarino, Deborah. *Is Your Mamma a Llama?* Illustrated by Steven Kellogg. New York, NY: Scholastic Incorporated, 1989.

Holabird, Katharine. *Alexander and the Magic Boat.* Illustrated by Helen Craig. New York, NY: Random House, 1990.

Kitamura, Satoshi. *Sheep in Wolves' Clothing.* New York, NY: Farrar, Straus and Giroux, 1995.

Lansky, Bruce, ed. *Kids Pick the Funniest Poems.* Illustrated by Steve Carpenter. New York, NY: Meadowbrook Press, 1991.

Mazer, Anne. *The Salamander Room.* Illustrated by Steve Johnson. New York, NY: Dragonfly Books, 1991.

Munsch, Robert. *Love You Forever.* Illustrated by Sheila McGraw. Willowdale, Ontario, Canada: A Firefly Book, 1986.

Parish, Peggy. *Amelia Bedelia*. Columbus, OH: Newfield Publications, Incorporated, 1963.

Parish, Peggy. *Thank You, Amelia Bedelia*. Pictures by Barbara Seibel Thomas. Columbus, OH: Newfield Publications, Incorporated, 1964.

Prelutsky, Jack. *The Baby Uggs are Hatching*. Illustrated by James Stevenson. New York, NY: Morrow, 1989.

Prelutsky, Jack. *My Parents Think I'm Sleeping*. Illustrated by Yossi Abolafia. New York, NY: Greenwillow Books, 1985.

Prelutsky, Jack. *The Pack Rat's Day*. Illustrated by Margaret Bloy Graham. New York, NY: McMillan Books, 1974.

Prelutsky, Jack. *What I Did Last Summer*. New York, NY: Greenwillow Books, 1984.

Prelutsky, Jack, compiler. *For Laughing Out Louder: More Poems to Tickle Your Funnybone*. Pictures by Marjorie Priceman. New York, NY: Alfred A. Knopf, 1995.

Pulver, Robin. *Mrs. Toggle's Zipper*. Illustrated by R. W. Alley. New York, NY: Four Winds Press, 1990.

Read-Along Rhymes: For the Very Young. Selected by Jack Prelutsky and illustrated by Mark Brown. New York, NY: Alfred A. Knopf, 1986.

Sendack, Maurice. *Where the Wild Things Are*. New York, NY: HarperTrophy, 1963.

Silverstein, Shel. *A Giraffe and a Half*. New York, NY: Harper Rowe, 1964.

Silverstein, Shel. *The Giving Tree*. New York, NY: Harper Rowe, 1964.

Silverstein, Shel. *A Light in the Attic*. New York, NY: Harper Rowe, 1974.

Silverstein, Shel. *Where The Sidewalk Ends*. New York, NY: Harper Rowe, 1974.

Waddell, Martin. *Can't You Sleep Little Bear?* Illustrated by Barbara Firth. Cambridge, MA: Candlewick Press, 1992.

Young, Selina. *Adam Pig's Everything Fun Book*. New York, NY: Delacorte Press, 1995.

Creativity

Ayan, Jordan. *Aha! 10 Ways to Free Your Creative Spirit and Find Your Great Ideas*. New York, NY: Crown Publishing Company, 1997.

Boostrom, Robert. *Developing Creative and Critical Thinking: An Integrated Approach.* Lincolnwood, IL: National Textbook Company, 1992.

Nierenberg, Gerard L. *The Art of Creative Thinking.* New York, NY: Simon & Schuster, 1982.

Oech, Roger von. *A Whack on the Side of the Head: How to Unlock Your Mind for Innovation.* Menlo Park, CA: Creative Think, 1983.

Optimism, Mindfulness, and Joy

Borysenko, Joan. *Fire in the Soul: A New Psychology of Spiritual Optimism.* New York, NY: Warner Books, 1993.

Cousins, Norman. *Head First: The Biology of Hope.* New York, NY: E.P. Dutton, 1989.

Gordon, Sol, and Harold Brecher. *Life is Uncertain . . . Eat Dessert First!: Finding the Joy You Deserve.* New York, NY: Dell Books, 1996.

Kabat-Zinn, Jon. *Full Catastrophe Living: Using the Wisdom of Your Body and Mind to Face Stress, Pain, and Illness.* New York, NY: Delacorte Press, 1990.

Kabat-Zinn, Jon. *Wherever You Go, There You Are: Mindfulness Meditation in Everyday Life.* New York, NY: Hyperion, 1994.

Seligman, Martin E. P. *Learned Optimism.* New York, NY: Alfred A. Knopf, 1991.

Seligman, Martin E. P. *The Optimistic Child: A Proven Program to Safeguard Children Against Depression and Build Lifelong Resilience.* New York, NY: HarperCollins, 1996.

Children and Stress

Davidson, Jeff. *Breathing Space: Living and Working at a Comfortable Pace in a Sped-Up Society.* New York, NY: MasterMedia Limited, 1991.

Elkind, David. *The Hurried Child: Growing Up Too Fast Too Soon.* Reading, MA: Addison-Wesley Publishing Company, Incorporated, 1988.

Humphrey, James H. *Children and Stress: Theoretical Perspectives and Recent Research.* New York, NY: AMS Press, 1988.

Youngs, Bettie B. *Stress and Your Child: Helping Kids Cope with the Strains and Pressures of Life.* New York, NY: Fawcett Columbine, 1995.

Theory and Research on Humor and Children

Joubert, Laurent. *Treatise on Laughter.* Translated and annotated by Gregory David De Rocher. Tuscaloosa, AL: University of Alabama Press, 1980.

McGhee, Paul E. *Humor: Its Origin and Development.* San Francisco, CA: W.H. Freeman, 1979.

McGhee, Paul E., and Antony J. Chapman, eds. *Children's Humour.* New York, NY: John Wiley & Sons, 1980.

Vaillant, George E. *The Wisdom of the Ego.* Cambridge, MA: Harvard University Press, 1993.

Woffenstein, Martha. *Children's Humor: A Psychological Analysis.* Bloomington, IN: Indiana University Press, 1978.

Ziv, Avner. *Personality and Sense of Humor.* New York, NY: Springer Publishing Company, 1984.

CHILDREN AND PARENT'S MAGAZINES

American Girl
Animals
Boys Life
Calliope
Chicadee for Young People
Child Life
Children's Television Workshop—Contact
Crayola Kids
FamilyFun
Highlights for Children
Humpty Dumpty's Magazine
Ladybug
Jack and Jill
National Geographic World
New Moon   The Magazine for Girls and their Parents
Odyssey—Science That's Out of this World
Owl—The Discovery Magazine for Kids
Pack-O-Fun
Parenting
Parents

Plays—Magazine for Young People
Ranger Rick—National Wildlife Federation
Scholastic Choice
Scholastic Science World
Sesame Street Parents
Spark—Creative Fun for Kids
Spider—The Magazine for Children
Sports Illustrated for Kids
Storyworks
Turtle
U.S. Kids—A Weekly Reader Magazine
Working Mother
Your Big Backyard—National Wildlife Federation
Zoobooks

THE INTERNET

Humor

Alan's Original Humor Archive
American Association of Therapeutic Humor
Best of: Humor
Comedy Central
Humor
The Humor House
Humor Database
Jest for the Health of It
The LaughPage
Oracle Service Humor Archive
Randolph's Humor Archive
Tina's Humor Archives

Parenting and Family

American Academy of Child and Adolescent Psychiatry
The CyberMom Dot Com
Family.com
FamilyPC

Family Surf
Family Time
Fathering Magazine
National Parent Information Network
Parents Place.com
Parent's Soup

Children's Literature—Resources for Parents

Books Every Child Should Read
Choosing a Child's Book
Family Planet
The Fluency Through Fables Index
Internet Public Library Story Hour
Parents and Children Together Online
ParentsPlace Reading Room
Read to Me

Children's Sites

A Girl's World Online Clubhouse
Angela and Rebekah's Fun Site for Kids
Astronomical Images Archive
Barbie Collectibles
Benny Goodsport and the Goodsport Gang
Bill Nye The Science Guy's Nye Labs Online
Brain Games
B.J. Pinchbeck's Homework Helper
Children's Concert Calendar
Children's Literature Web Guide
Children's Software Review
Club Girl Tech
Cinet's Games Center
Concertina Publishing
CTW Online—The Official Home of Sesame Street
Cyberkids
Cyberspace Middle School
Discovery Channel Online
Dr. Fellowbug's Laboratory of Fun and Horror
Electronic Zoo/Netvet

Eureka!
Exploranet
Exploratorium
Field Museum
Fourkids Treehouse
Freezone
Games Domain
Geocities Enchanted Forest Neighborhood
Global Show-n-Tell Museum
Goosebumps on the Web
Gurl
Gustown
Happy Puppy's Worldwide Web Page for Youngsters
Headbone Interactive
Headbone Wizard of Oz Club
Is That a Fact?
Kid's after School Clubhouse
Kid's Planet
Kidstar
Mystery Critter Crunch Adventure
Nine Planets
Planet Troll
Sea World/Busch Gardens Animal Information Database
Seussville
TheKids.com
Theodore Tugboat Activity Center
The Ultimate Children's Internet Sites
Worldvillage Kidz
Yazone
Web-A-Sketch

Children's On-Line Magazines

American Girl
Cyberschool Magazine
First Cut
Midlink Magazine
Splash Kids
Sports Illustrated for Kids

I wish you and your family well as you explore the vast world
of humor, play, and laughter. I welcome you to write me
to share funny moments, stories of your children,
playful encounters, silly experiences, family cartoons,
or anything that promotes the joy of family life.

I can be reached at:

25 NORTH WAHSATCH, SUITE 101
COLORADO SPRINGS, CO 80903